GERMANY:
KEY TO PEACE
IN EUROPE

Volumes in This Series

GERMANY

KEY TO PEACE
IN EUROPE

by

KARL BRANDT

Food Research Institute
Stanford University

Foreword by
HAROLD W. BRADLEY

CLAREMONT, CALIFORNIA

1949

CONTENTS

FOREWORD

THE lectures here presented in book form constitute
the tenth volume in the series relating to public
affairs sponsored annually by the Associated Colleges
at Claremont. Since 1942, each of these annual vol-
umes has dealt with some aspect of international affairs.
The colleges, in planning the lectures for 1949, followed the pattern which has now become virtually an
established tradition.

The 1949 lectures were delivered by Dr. Karl
Brandt, professor of agricultural economics in the
Food Research Institute, Stanford University, who selected as his subject, "Germany: Key to Peace in
Europe." It will be recognized that the subject of
these lectures has far reaching implications for the
most baffling of our contemporary political problems—
the maintenance of peace with freedom. Indeed, it
may be regarded as the central issue now confronting
the western world for, as Dr. Brandt so clearly proves,
the fate of Europe is inextricably linked to the revival
of economic activity and political sanity in Germany.
It is also a subject involving a host of controversial
issues, which often are discussed with more emotion
or bias than with a calm and scholarly appraisal. This
is not strange. To millions of persons in this country

and in Europe, Germany is still synonymous with "the German problem"; and the fear of future German aggression and the lingering suspicion that the ideologies of National Socialism did not die with Hitler continue to disturb many who are in a position to influence the judgments of the peoples of this country and of western Europe. It is the more important, therefore, that those who can assess the situation calmly, who are intimately informed as to the present developments and prospects within Germany, and whose reputation for objective analysis of economic facts merit confidence should share with the public their judgment as to the present conditions and long term realities involved in the reconstruction of Germany.

So rapidly have events moved that much of what appears in the chapter on American policy is already history. To a lesser extent, a similar situation prevails with respect to the other two chapters. But it is living history, vitally affecting events and decisions today and related by one who has observed this history as it unfolded. These lectures will also have the greatest interest for the future historian, who will find in them a primary source of real value for the understanding of the problems faced by the victors and of the policies they adopted. For the greatest number of readers, however, these lectures will be primarily important as a frank and thoughtful discussion of recent policy and of current issues which must be met and solved intelligently if disaster is to be avoided.

Dr. Brandt is unusually well qualified to discuss critically the questions related to the economic rehabilitation of Germany. He is a native of that country, was educated in German universities, was a member of the faculty of the College of Agriculture at the University of Berlin from 1929 to 1933, and served several agencies of the government of Germany as an economic adviser prior to the advent of Hitler to power. He came to the United States in 1933; and has been a member of the faculty of Stanford University since 1938. He is now a citizen of the United States. During and since the war he has frequently served the government and people of his adopted country, particularly as an adviser on problems relating to German economy; and most recently he has been an economic adviser to the United States Office for Military Government for Germany.

From the beginning in 1940, this lecture series has been made possible by the generous support of a group of business and professional men in Los Angeles and vicinity. It is with genuine pleasure and gratitude that the colleges make public acknowledgment of their debt to these public spirited persons—a debt which is shared by all who recognize the need for such scholarly and critical analyses of current issues as are presented in the lectures of Dr. Brandt.

HAROLD W. BRADLEY

Claremont, California
August 15, 1949

I.
AMERICAN FOREIGN POLICY
TOWARD GERMANY

AMERICAN FOREIGN POLICY
TOWARD GERMANY

THE foreign relations of the United States, the world's leading power, concern a great many nations—those of the western hemisphere, of Asia, Africa, and of Europe. Yet, while it seems quite out of proportion in terms of her area, population, or economic resources, Germany has, for more than 30 years, occupied one of the most prominent places within the range of our foreign policy.

Four years after the unconditional surrender of the last remnants of the Wehrmacht, Germany does not even formally exist as a nation. Large parts of her area, such as Alsace-Lorraine, the Saar, and half of East Prussia have been annexed by the victors. From still larger parts, all Germans have been expelled and the territory has been settled with other nationals. The remainder, less than three-fourths of her original area, enveloping about 68 million people, is occupied by the armies of four major occupation powers, with the area and the people split into two mutually blockaded compartments separated by the Iron Curtain. Technically, a state of war between the occupying powers and the German people still exists, in the absence of a declaration of peace or even an armistice.

Notwithstanding this situation, the importance of the German desk in the State Department is today perhaps even greater than it was when Germany ranked as one of the world's foremost powers, or when her armies were on the rampage. German affairs happen to be the most hotly contested ground between the United States, Great Britain, and France on the one hand, and Soviet Russia on the other. And even in the negotiations between the three Western allies, Germany looms large as an area of dissention and dispute.

Historically a great many friendly relations and ties have existed between the American people and the Germans. The names of Baron von Steuben, the drillmaster of George Washington's army, and of Carl Schurz highlight the participation of Germans in shaping American democracy. Millions of German farmers have helped to settle this country, particularly in Pennsylvania and the Middle West. After the failure of their Revolution of 1848, hundreds of thousands of democratic Germans came to America, to become loyal and esteemed citizens. Their talented minds joined the northern leadership in the Civil War and contributed to the victory of the Union. German higher education, particularly in universities, contributed substantially to the rise of American institutions of higher learning. The broad development of scientific research and its application to modern industry in Germany have had decisive influence on the power and depth of the industrial revolution in this country. Aside from these intellectual ties, German private capital helped to build the American railroads between 1870 and 1914. The map of the United States is sprinkled with German names, as are telephone books and the rosters of top-ranking military officers, scholars, and statesmen.

These well-known connections between the two nations notwithstanding, the dominant historical fact of this generation is that the United States defeated Germany in World War I at sea, in the air, and on land, and in World War II annihilated her military might and utterly destroyed the nation. On both occasions, our Congress delayed making the fateful decision to throw the nation's strength against Germany. War was not declared until April of 1917, and in World War II, the Congress declared war after Germany had done so, and at a time when it was almost too late to prevent irreparable losses.

War was declared in 1917 because it was feared that after Germany defeated England and France on the western front, her navy would rule the Atlantic. In 1941 the motive was essentially the same, but far more compelling, because at that time control had fallen into the hands of a gang of ruthless brigands, who had, under their indiscernibly insane leader, first enslaved the German people before expanding its tyranny by military conquest over most of the European continent, and was threatening to go beyond.

This course of events—particularly with the precedent of Napoleon's tyranny over Europe—would not comprise a particularly complex chapter in modern history. Nor was it unique that within 24 years, war was again undertaken against the same nation. History abounds in illustrations of repetitive wars between the same nations. What makes the historical record of American foreign policy toward Germany uniquely interesting, and charges the complex relations between the two nations with every element of human conflict, tragic war, and interdependence is the fact that after having defeated her in 1918, the United States not only granted relief to the German population, but also that American private capital to a large extent financed Germany's economic reconstruction. The aid of $13 billion in American loans and American support of the revision of the reparations program were favorable to the rise of the Weimar Republic to a position of leadership on the Continent. At present, four years after having destroyed practically all of Germany's important cities—70 in number—the government of the United States is once more engaged in the infinitely complex task of rebuilding Germany as a nation and a state.

This is an astounding performance in view of the fact that during the war and immediately after the fighting ceased, military action and diplomatic proceedings were clearly oriented toward the goal of ridding the United States and the world once and for all of the nuisance of Germany. She was to be disposed of as a military or economic power and as a political factor in world affairs. When, however, the last remnants of her military power had surrendered and were interned, when her cities were smoldering ruins and her catastrophe-stricken population completely prostrate, Germany turned out to be an even greater problem than ever; and within the span of a few months it became inescapably necessary for our policy toward her to be turned from annihilation back again to reconstruction.

To what extent this new course can and will succeed is one of the most intriguing problems in the foreign affairs of our time. While some of the contours of a new Germany are already discernible, it is certain that the Soviet Union, in its determined drive toward the total absorption of Europe and Asia, will not spare any effort to induce us to alter our course and prevent the reconstruction of Germany and her integration into the Atlantic community.

To understand the present situation and to form sound judgments on the German issue, one must thoroughly analyze the origin and implication of the policy of annihilation, together with the reasons for its complete reversal. We must retrace the steps taken by our civil and military authorities, trying to understand the psychological atmosphere that prevailed when the various decisions were made. In so doing, we shall avoid the mistake of assuming that decisions about future living conditions for other nations, or about the security of our own people are exclusively the result of cold, rational erudition or a consensus of the wisdom of statesmen cooperating in the noble task of building a lasting peace for all the people on this earth. In examining this complex record, we quickly learn that even here in this great democracy of ours, history is made by men—men who wield great power, sometimes a very few men, if not one—and that men are fallible and sometimes do act under the impact of emotions as well as their rational capacities, and follow expediency rather than principle. But we also find out, and may take comfort from it, that under the democracy in this country, it is always possible for the nation to correct errors and to change its course. The results of errors in our foreign policy do not vanish overnight, and some of them prove to be very costly errors, but we can change the course of human events for ourselves and for others.

From 1933 through 1945 and even later, the problem of Germany was identical with the problem of the Nazi state—so far as our foreign policy was concerned. Our government dealt with the Nazi state in terms of our tradition not to interfere with the internal affairs of other countries. This made it pragmatically difficult to keep clearly in mind the probability that the Nazi regime might be no more than a phase in German history and, one might even say, a manifestation of but one sort of conduct and the predilection of a specific type of Germans. But, in the course of time, any distinction between the nature of the long-run problem posed by the geographic location and historical position of the German people in the European economic and political picture and the temporary problems raised by the tyrant and his vicious regime faded out.

Much good will existed between the Weimar Republic and America in all public relations up to and through the time when the Weimar Republic was desperately struggling to free itself from the grip of the economic depression. The picture changed rapidly in 1933. Franklin Roosevelt moved into the White House at the same time Hitler took over in Germany. In less than a year, relations between Germany and the United States began to be recklessly and deliberately poisoned on the German side. The lawlessness of the new regime was clearly demonstrated from the very beginning. On June 30, 1934, hundreds of people, including the former chancellor, Schleicher, and his wife were foully murdered in cold blood. It thus was plain that the regime operated with ruthlessness and brutality, and its victims were Germans. The following years up to 1937, were marked by the Hitler-engineered assassination of Austria's chancellor Dollfuss, the re-introduction of conscription, the formation of the Berlin-Rome-Tokyo axis, the re-militarization of the Rhineland, and the speeding up of German rearmament. These acts left no room for doubt about the aggressive designs of the Nazi regime.

Yet in the face of these facts, the British government under Chamberlain, and the French cabinet under Daladier were firmly set on a course of appeasement. In Britain and America, too, economists for years had been building up a case for the Nazi state's economic weakness and the collapse of any major enterprise that Hitler's armies might undertake. While the American public became more and more alarmed and unfriendly toward the Nazi regime, particularly because of its vicious discrimination against German Jews, America was also reluctant to face the dangerous issue squarely, and for the most part public opinion supported a policy of neutrality. Pacifists and isolationists led the discussions about foreign affairs in the committees of the House and the Senate.

The popular determinist theory that the Nazi economy was drifting into bankruptcy, and that therefore any large-scale military venture would be impeded was a welcome narcotic for the American business world. It detested the idea of having to face a war, in spite of assertions by Senator Nye and others that American industry was mongering for war. The escapist, pseudo-economic fiction about the Nazi economy was strengthened by large numbers of exiles from

Germany who failed completely to understand the inner mechanics of 20th-century totalitarianism. They did not grasp its potentialities economically, politically, or militarily. Together with most of the observers and analysts in the English-speaking world, they did not see that the totalitarian state is economically a per-petual-motion engine which can produce almost any effect it wants to within the boundaries of its technical limits. It can expand and allocate output to the state's purposes because it can arbitrarily curtail civilian con-sumption or private investment toward civilian ends. Politically such a regime can endure forever, irrespec-tive of opposton from within, so long as the secret-police machinery maintains its efficiency and operates with extreme brutality. A revolution or coup d'état has a chance only if the army joins it and overpowers the secret police. Otherwise, such regimes collapse only when they clash with and are defeated by outside forces. Militarily it was not clearly recognized that by virtue of despotism and absolute command, a totali-tarian state at war with democratic states would have the advantage of initiative and surprise in aggression, and the opportunity of supplementing resources by speedy occupation.

These failures in protective perception were the re-sult of the insistence of democratic peoples upon being left alone to pursue civilian happiness up to the very point at which war becomes inescapably necessary to self-defense against deadly peril. Any sort of plausible theory to that end—no matter how disastrously wrong —was powerfully attractive.

So it was that a thousand opportunities to bring the sinister forces in Germany to a full stop were wasted. From 1934 to 1937 no serious effort to stop Hitler was made, although no risk of a major war was yet involved. But even in 1937 and 1938, when the sand in the hour-glass of peace began to fall lower and lower, no decisive action was taken.

One little country, living precariously under the shadow of the tyrant, decided in 1936 to defend the freedom of its citizens; in that year Switzerland spent $350 million on national defense, put demolition charges in the tunnels through the Alps, determined to blow them up and to fight for every inch of land if necessary. Had England and France spent a proportional amount on national defense, and in the same spirit, there would not have been the sort of war that ensued two years later. If the United States had built up a defense system in 1936 and had made it abundantly clear that this defense system would come to the rescue of France and England if they were attacked, there could not have been a second world war.

Instead, after Austria was annexed, we had Munich. France and Great Britain thrust Czechoslovakia into Nazi slavery, surrendering an 80-division first-class Czech army, tilting the military scales on the Continent in Hitler's favor by 160 divisions. Neither France nor Great Britain at that time had armies even approaching in size or equipment the Czech forces donated to the Nazis to secure "peace in our time."

In the meantime, Franklin Roosevelt and his cabinet were kept well abreast of everything that was happening in the Third Reich from the very beginning. Yet no plans commensurate with the rapidly precipitating danger of war by Axis initiative were even proposed. The common explanation for this situation is that any notion of large-scale armament was academic because American public opinion had not reached the point where such a program could have been accepted. This explanation is not a satisfactory one, because in a democracy informed leaders have the right to share with the people what they know, and thus bring to bear upon critical issues the force of enlightened public opinion. But if, for the sake of argument, one accepts the doubtful view that from 1933 to 1937 American public opinion reasonably fostered the country's military weakness, all the more reason was there for the diplomatic service to compensate for that temporary weakness by launching an offensive against aggression through its own channels. This, if I am not mistaken, is the real meaning of diplomacy and the job of the statesman.

One of the well-known events that was transpiring in the Third Reich at the time the Nazi regime was building its super-mobile army, tank divisions, and a supporting air force, was a concerted opposition to Hitler on the part of the German general staff, composed of professional soldiers with a conservative political philosophy. Generals Beck, von Hammerstein, von Fritsch, and Halder led this opposition and considered Hitler's plans of aggression as reckless ventures. These generals had even plotted to arrest Hitler and his henchmen and to negotiate with the western powers—a plot nipped in the bud by Chamberlain's visit to Berchtesgaden and Hitler's triumph at Munich. Competent diplomacy, armed with these facts, required that the cards be resourcefully played into the hands of the German Resistance, which, with proper aid from the outside, could have prevented the use of the German army for aggression.

Recourse to the concept of non-interference in the internal affairs of other nations, cited in the memoirs of our statesmen, has a hollow sound of abdication and denial of the possibility of saving the lives of American soldiers and the strength and wealth of many nations by appropriate and intelligent cooperation with men of influence and ability who were willing to risk torture and death to prevent the disaster being brewed in their own country. Alert and resourceful diplomacy would certainly have called for all-out concentration upon the task of strengthening the opposition to Hitler and encouraging it to restore government by law.

The German Resistance was represented by infinitely more people than members of the general staff. It consisted of a number of groups of responsible Germans, representing all classes, professions, shades of political view, and leaders of both churches. They spoke for a genuine elite of highly civilized Europeans of democratic convictions who despised Hitler and his gangster regime as much as did any American or Englishman. This group plotted against Hitler while in the grip of the Gestapo. Even before the war, the leading figures in the Resistance had been known for what they were, not only in Washington, but in London and some other capitals as well. In the summer of 1939, one of them, Goerdeler, with the approval of the generals who opposed Hitler's plans, visited England, America, and France, presenting highest officials with information on the internal situation in Germany. Others, like von Trott zu Solz, Pechel, Kordt, and von Schlabrendorff contacted the British Foreign Office and American officials in connection with a possible coup d'état. In May, 1942, two prominent members of the Resistance, pastor Bonhoeffer and Dr. Schoenfeld, formerly of the ecumenical council of churches in Geneva, met in Sweden with the Bishop of Chichester and handed him a list of the leading conspirators against Hitler for the attention of Anthony Eden.[1] The

---

[1] Hans Rothfels, *The German Opposition to Hitler* (Hinsdale, Ill., 1948), pp. 140-41.

question of whether the Allies would be willing to deal with a bona fide German government after the overthrow of the Hitler regime was raised, and a possible treaty of peace was outlined. This proposed peace settlement included: (1) the withdrawal of all German forces from all occupied countries; (2) reparations for damages; (3) complete destruction of the Nazi regime; (4) the execution of Hitler, Himmler, Goebbels, and the leaders of the Gestapo, the SS, and the SA; and (5) the formation of a decentralized Germany governed by law and social justice.

Mr. Eden remarked that some of the names of the conspirators were known at the Foreign Office and that similar peace feelers had reached him via neutral countries and that he would take the matter under consideration. On July 17 he informed the Bishop that no action could be taken. The Resistance leaders continued to make efforts to obtain a sign of Allied willingness to deal with them after a revolution. These efforts, which grew in intensity and daring until a few days before the invasion, were invariably turned down flat in Washington and London. Contacts with the Resistance were kept alive until the end by our intelligence, but merely from the standpoint of how much the Resistance would weaken the battlefronts.

In fact, as soon as the war began, the attitude toward Germany had quickly hardened to the principle that no differential treatment was desirable for any of her citizens and hence no negotiations were possible or desirable. Wrath over the crimes of the Nazi regime was turned against all Germans, and was precipitated in the formula of collective guilt—a formula that betrays all Christian tenets of democracy and is based on a complete lack of understanding of the totalitarian state.

One is drawn to the conclusion that the policy of diplomatic appeasement and acquiescence in the face of flagrant violations of all the principles of civilized forms of government by law in effect amounted to interference in the internal affairs of another people. This is particularly apparent in light of the American concept of conspiracy which we introduced in the Nüremberg trials and have made a new foundation of international law. In his report to the President about the prosecution of war criminals, Mr. Justice Jackson stated.[2]

> Early in the Nazi regime, people of this country came to look upon the Nazi Government as not constituting a legitimate state pursuing the legitimate objective of a member of the international community. They came to view the Nazis as a band of brigands, set on subverting within Germany every vestige of a rule of law which would entitle an aggregation of people to be looked upon collectively as a member of the family of nations. Our people were outraged by the oppressions, the cruelest forms of torture, the large-scale murder, and

---

[2] U. S. Dept. State, *Department of State Bulletin*, June 10, 1945, p. 1075.

the wholesale confiscation of property which initialed the Nazi regime within Germany. They witnessed persecution of the greatest enormity on religious, political and racial grounds, the breakdown of trade unions, and the liquidation of all religious and moral influences.

Now, if we proceed to punish summarily *ex post* the perpetration of such a conspiracy, would it not then follow that it would also have been our obligation to act through diplomatic cooperation with people determined to risk their lives to counteract the conspiracy? In the absence of either energetic armament or diplomatic moves to check the aggression from the inside, Hitler was encouraged to feel that he would be fairly safe in running the risk of war. When the Wehrmacht started to roll west, supplied with raw materials by the Soviets, neither France nor England had defenses on the Continent to match it. The United States was in no way prepared for war and was not yet of a mind to enter as an active belligerent. Escapist day-dreaming took the center of attention still; winning the war was supposed to be possible by means of a long-range war of attrition—that is, by economic strangulation with the blockade. No intellectual acrobatics decorated with statistics were too far-fetched if only they served to prove that by a shortage of phosphate fertilizers or something else, the Nazis could be starved out at a safe distance and forced to desert their Continental fortress. Realists who understood the totalitarian state had

known from the beginning that this streamlined tyranny could be destroyed only by direct attack with su-
perior forces on land, sea, and in the air—and the
sooner the better.

This record of neglect in the proper and timely prep-
aration for the military contest has not been entirely
or without loss compensated by the gigantic effort we
made when finally we were forced to declare war on
Germany and Japan, though we like to assume the
contrary. The element of loss enters in because our
present dilemma is largely the direct result of our
initial unpreparedness. The fact that now we have no
peace, several years after having successfully waged
World War II, and are by no means sure that another
even more crucial test will not come at any moment, is
due largely to our lag in getting ready. It is also due
to our unwillingness or inability to use diplomacy as a
refined but powerful tool of foreign policy in dealing
with individuals and groups within Germany before
and during the war, and even later.

Having overrun Poland, Norway, the Lowlands,
and France, Hitler made the fatal mistake of attacking
Soviet Russia. This event had complex repercussions;
from that point on, right up to the present instant of
time, it was impossible to speak of foreign policy toward Germany apart from foreign policy toward the
Soviet Union. The attack induced the British and
their allies to unite with the Soviet power, and the

United States to extend to Soviet Russia the material aid previously offered to all nations who would fight against the Axis. When we actively entered the war in December, 1941, we became an ally of the Soviet Union, and this relationship was the central element in the joint British-American effort to destroy the Wehrmacht and to liberate the nations it had conquered. The enemy was proving to be so strong and his surprise tactics so effective that every additional division that could be put into the field against him was more than welcome, and the Soviets had plenty of divisions.

The emergency arising from our "too little, too late" procedures forced us into an alliance with the totalitarian power that twice had attacked Finland, in complicity with the Nazi brigands had divided Poland, and had annexed the three Baltic states. This alliance with Soviet Russia was entered into as a logical matter of military expedience, but it soon became evident that immeasurably more was involved than just a military alliance; indeed, it began to have an ever-increasing influence on our foreign policy, as may be illustrated by the deadlocked United Nations Organization and the precarious situation in the cold war at this moment.

Of course, the Soviet rulers needed our military help as much as we and the British needed theirs. Our goal was the destruction of the Wehrmacht and the removal of aggressive totalitarianism, German and Japanese styles. Stalin and his associates never lost sight of the fact for a single moment that for them the war was only a transitional phase of their own private long-range plans in foreign affairs. The rugged endurance of the Russian people in defense of their homeland called forth our admiration. Under the impact of powerful propaganda to that end, the American public's attitude toward the Soviet government also became cordial, and the supposed social and economic achievements of that regime were interpreted as those of a good-neighbor democracy. It was not the American public alone that for several years enjoyed the pleasant sensation of a world united in friendship as soon as the aggressors were defeated. Many of our statesmen and generals, under Franklin Roosevelt's leadership, also believed there existed a sort of community of interest and spirit of friendship between the United States and Russia. This psychological atmosphere profoundly influenced the course of our foreign policy toward Germany, and contributed its share to the ultimate conclusion of friendly cooperation with the Soviets.

Characteristically in America, our major relations with other nations are accompanied by heavy groundswells of public emotion and sentiment which temporarily black out our knowledge of history and cold facts. In Soviet Russia there is neither the need nor the opportunity for that kind of support for the Kremlin's diplomatic moves. While official acts in our foreign policy are ordinarily preceded and accompanied by extensive public discussion and reflect all the possible motivations, Soviet moves emerge from the walls closeting the deliberations of the Politbureau and often enough have the world pondering for months what the motives or the real goals may have been.

For her military pursuits Russia obtained from the United States and Great Britain a maximum amount of food and ordnance, and priority in Western joint-chiefs-of-staff plans for amphibious attack in Africa and the Mediterranean, and she also managed to have abandoned the assault on the Continental fortress through the Balkans in favor of one from the west or the northwest. Of all the major decisions made during the war, none had greater political consequences than this one, for it put the Western forces on the Continent at the point farthest from the eastern front, leaving all of eastern and central Europe an operational area for the Red Army. It is not for me to weigh the military merits of this decision. But in discussing our foreign policy toward Europe and Germany, it is essential to acknowledge the fact that by virtue of that momentous decision, the opportunity for Russian expansion toward the west was prepared. As early as December, 1941, Russia began to lay out her demands that the borders she had before Hitler's attack on her be restored. In other words, Russia sought recognition for the annexations she had made during the time her pact with Hitler was in force. These included claims to the three Baltic States, to Poland east of the Curzon Line, and to parts of Finland and Rumania. At the same time, Stalin indicated that he wanted East Prussia transferred to Poland and the Rhineland and Bavaria set up as independent states. Our Department of State resisted and sidetracked the issue until the Yalta conference took it up in February, 1945. This early revelation of Soviet territorial ambitions demonstrates the continuity of Russia's plans to alter the political geography of Europe, dating back to her collaboration in Hitler's aggression.

In his report to the Secretary of War on September 1, 1945, Chief of Staff General George C. Marshall said:[3]

> At that time [April, 1942] the Red Army was slowly falling back under the full fury of the German assault, and it was accepted at the London Conference that everything practicable must be done to reduce the pressure on the Soviet lest she collapse and the door be opened wide for a complete conquest of Europe and a probable juncture with the Japanese in the Indian Ocean.

This apprehension began to lessen to some extent with the Russian victory at Stalingrad toward the end of 1942, but essentially it lasted until the summer of 1943.

---

[3] U. S. War Department, *Biennial Report of the Chief of Staff of the United States Army to the Secretary of War, July 1, 1943, to June 30, 1945* (Washington, 1945) p. 8.

By October, 1943, over half of the territory the Soviets had lost since June, 1941, was re-occupied. By that time the possibility of a peace between Soviet Russia and Nazi Germany loomed ominously on the horizon.

The historic conference at Teheran in November, 1943, brought together Roosevelt, Churchill, and Stalin, and Stalin succeeded in getting most of the assurances and concessions he wanted. We attached no conditions to our enormous accessions to Stalin's demand for material lend-lease support and adaptations in military strategy. The mystery behind this unconditional blank endorsement had its roots in several circumstances. The American armed forces had still not reached maximum striking power, and the vast manpower of the Red Army was needed to hold as many German divisions on the eastern front as possible.

Moreover, after the alliance with Russia became effective, it was considered dangerous to harmonious relations with her to maintain contact with Resistance groups in Germany. Refusal to strengthen these respectable efforts to accomplish a costly war's goal by the effective use of diplomacy originated in the determination of Franklin Roosevelt and influential men around him not to be tricked by any Germans into a negotiated peace and diverted from the goal of meting out summary punishment to the German nation for the dastardly deeds of its criminal government. This was formally codified by Roosevelt's declaration of the policy of unconditional surrender at the Casablanca conference in January, 1943. Secretary Hull and the State Department were as much surprised by this declaration as were Churchill and the British Foreign Office. Nine months later, when the question of a joint declaration to the German people on the basis of unconditional surrender came up at Teheran, Stalin informed Roosevelt that he considered it bad tactics toward Germany, and recommended instead that specific terms be made to the German people.

Unconditional surrender had exactly the effect anticipated by Secretary Hull. The German army fought long beyond the point where further battle had become senseless, and the victorious armies did have to take over all the jobs of national, provincial, and local government as well as the task of building a sort of provisional substitute for a German government. The very worst effect of the iron-clad unconditional surrender formula was, however, never mentioned in any discussions. It rendered the task for the German Resistance almost hopeless, because it was made plain that no matter how thoroughly a coup d'état or a bloody revolution might rid the country of the Nazi regime, and regardless of how far a new government might be willing to go in meeting the demands of victimized nations, it would get neither a hearing nor even a chance for an armistice.

Psychologically the whole concept of unconditional surrender demonstrated that the wisdom of moderation in making peace and the will to adhere to the principles of the Atlantic Charter had already been washed overboard by the powerful sway of negative emotions. It proved that on the Anglo-American side, at least, it was a matter of complete indifference whether a desirable form of government, the restoration of law, the reparation of damages or the punishment of the Nazi leaders were brought about by German initiative and revolt against the despot. The underlying assumption was simply that 67 million people in one of the world's most advanced industrial nations would for a generation or for 50 years be subject to the dictate of the conqueror—victors who, because of the criminal acts committed by the destroyed government, could do with the vanquished nation exactly as they pleased.

Remarkably enough, in the face of this hopeless isolation created by the doctrine of unconditional surrender, and despite the other rebuffs it had encountered throughout the Hitler regime from Britain and America, the German Resistance went doggedly ahead. Neither setbacks from the outside nor the terrible risks it continually faced at home prevented the Resistance from trying to kill Hitler on July 20, 1944, and overthrow the Nazi regime. That attempt failed, as had two earlier ones, and during the nine months that followed, the Gestapo arrested, tortured, and murdered most of the Resistance leaders. Thus ended the efforts of 168 of the men who in themselves had comprised the political leadership of a new peaceful and decent Germany. The absence of 168 outstanding men is a most tragic loss to our efforts in the reconstruction of Western Europe.

Unconditional surrender had another weakness in the philosophy that lay behind it. The implication was that the Allies were united and that their political goals in the countries subjected to the surrender were harmonious. This is paradoxical, because one of the things contributing to this blank and vague formula of omnipotence was the knowledge that attempts to reach agreement on specific conditions would widen the rift between the Soviet Union and the Western allies. The tacit assumption that Russia would be satisfied with any policy so long as it destroyed Germany as a power and more or less restored Russia to her pre-1933 status turned out to be a painful error.

The formal shaping of our post-victory foreign policy toward Germany began in 1944, when it became apparent that final victory was only a matter of time. It culminated in the Morgenthau Plan, the major outlines of which were conceived by the Secretary of the Treasury, and which was given specific form and content by Dr. Harry D. White and staff members of the Treasury, and support by Roosevelt and Hopkins against fierce opposition from the departments of State and War.

The Morgenthau Plan was a scheme of ruthless, undisguised vengeance and the most extreme effort made in the course of history to take permanent punitive action against a conquered nation. Specifically, it provided for the annexation of Silesia and half of East Prussia by Poland, annexation of the Saar and a large part of the Rhineland by France, and annexation of northern Schleswig-Holstein by Denmark. The rest of Germany was to be divided into three parts—a north and south German state and an international zone comprising the Ruhr and the west-German industrial area. This zone, the industrial heartland of Western Europe, was to be stripped of all industrial installations, the mines closed and flooded, and the area itself so controlled that at no time could it again be industrialized. Policing and control of the civil administration in Germany were to be turned over to all the nations Germany had once occupied.

While the two government departments chiefly concerned with the administration of Germany after defeat and the shaping of the future peace opposed the Morgenthau Plan, the Secretary of the Treasury discussed it with Mr. Churchill at Quebec, and in combination with negotiations on the continuation of lend-lease and a loan of $6 billion to Great Britain, the signatures of Churchill and Roosevelt were obtained on a memorandum drafted by Morgenthau in which it was agreed that Germany would be "pastoralized." One of the chief arguments used by the Treasury was the need to relieve Great Britain of German competition in the world market.

The staunch oppostion waged against this Carthaginian peace plan by the State and War departments led to early tempering of its most destructive elements, such as the complete destruction of the coal and steel industries of the Ruhr. Yet the essential idea of the plan, aside from its crude temper of blind vengeance, was a design to insure against further military ventures by eliminating economic war potential—the doctrine of de-militarization by de-industrialization. About 2,000 people in the Foreign Economic Administration worked out separate plans for the reduction of the important groups of German industries. The framework for these plans was a formula to which, in contradiction to all the principles for which he stood throughout the years, even Secretary Hull had subscribed; it provided that the living standard of the German people be held down to a subsistence level, irrespective of how hard they might work. Although Secretary Stimson opposed it, this American formula was later applied in all reparations and de-industrialization plans, and was incorporated in the Potsdam agreement. Morgenthau, strongly supported by Roosevelt, succeeded in forcing upon the departments of State and War a thorough revision of the directive to General Eisenhower on the treatment of the Germans. This instruction read in part:[4]

> Except as may be necessary to carry out these objectives [elimination of Nazism and militarism; enforcement of reparations and restitution program; protection of safety of occupying forces by preventing starvation or such disease and unrest as would endanger them; assumption of controls by German authorities, who are to bear, with the German people, full responsibility for administration thereof] *you will take no steps (a) toward the economic rehabilitation of Germany, or (b) designed to maintain or strengthen the Germany economy.*

While the directive was far less destructive than the Morgenthau Plan, its tenor was nevertheless negative.

The last conference at which some sort of strained agreement was reached concerning the treatment of Germany took place at Potsdam in July, 1945, although the Russians had unilaterally created the *fait accompli* of transferring to Poland a fourth of the German territory. With the Wehrmacht held at bay, the Red Army had taken Berlin and occupied all of eastern Germany up to the Elbe, and in line with a secret agreement made at Yalta, the American army had yielded to Soviet occupation the province and state of Saxony and Thuringia.

---

[4] U. S. Dept. State, *Department of State Bulletin*, Oct. 21, 1945, pp. 598, 601. Italics added.

At Potsdam the United States and Great Britain tried to save face by designating the transfer of German territory to Poland as only a temporary measure, and stipulated that the expulsion of the German population of that area be executed in a "humane and orderly manner." It was also agreed that the transfer to Germany of Germans remaining in Poland, Hungary, and Czechoslovakia would have to be undertaken. By these decisions Germany was reduced in territory by one-fourth, and from 12 to 13 million destitute expellees were forced into this smaller area. The main rift between the Soviets and the West during the conference came when Russia made new and exorbitant reparations demands from current German production; at Moscow the American view that reparations be taken only in the form of capital goods dismantled and transferred to recipient nations had prevailed. A compromise was reached, providing that by February, 1946, the four military governors would work out a plan setting forth a permissible level of industries for Germany to retain. The criterion for setting this level again was the formula of average living standards not to exceed the average of other European nations. In the negotiations that followed, the Russian delegates struggled tenaciously for the lowest possible level of industries, obviously to put a maximum number of industrial plants in the reparations pool. The Western powers met them halfway in order to secure the fulfillment of the decisive condition that Germany be treated as an economic unit, which had been set forth at Potsdam and agreed to by the Russians.

By the spring of 1946 it had become evident that the Russians were violating everything to which they had agreed at Potsdam; they refused to unify the four zones of occupation and were rapidly sovietizing their zone of Germany. An end to the era of cordial co-operation with Russia had finally come. When V. M. Molotov crowned his obstreperous tactics, which had vitiated any progress toward peace, by denouncing the level-of-industries plan and the idea of de-industrializing Germany at the Council of Foreign Ministers in Paris, the United States officially changed its policy toward Germany.

Molotov made a strong appeal to the Germans by openly attacking our whole policy of de-industrialization, although the Russian delegates had been responsible for the low level of industries. At the same time the Russian radio broadcast throughout Germany all the details of the Morgenthau Plan, and attacked it as the vicious vengeance of America. Thus the ally whom we had saved from disaster at the hands of the Wehrmacht at enormous sacrifice used the Treasury Department's old, ill-conceived plan as a key political weapon against us.

To counteract this, Secretary Byrnes went to Stuttgart and laid down a new course of foreign policy toward Germany, which has been pursued since then with increasing emphasis on sane reconstruction as originally evisaged by the departments of State and War. This new policy is now solidly embedded in the Truman Doctrine checking Soviet Russia's further expansion, in the Marshall Plan aiding the reconstruction of Europe, and in the Atlantic Pact. The new policy acknowledges the accomplished fact that for the time being the only part of Germany in which we and our Western allies have freedom of action is the three Western zones and the three Western sectors of Berlin. The new policy would establish a new federal state for Germany, granting to that state the power to reindustrialize and an opportunity to try to reach a new balance of trade rendering her close to 50 million people independent of foreign charity. Finally we freed ourselves from the illusion of a United Nations operating under the harmonious leadership of the Big Three.

Real reconstruction in Germany did not begin until the summer of 1948. Up to that time, our military government—on instructions from Washington—delayed final action on such important issues as currency reform, a constitution for the projected federal republic, and the formation of a federal government. It was felt necessary to keep the door open in that way for agreement with the Russians.

Aside from this top-level delay, coordination of

policies among the three Western military governments crept along at snail's pace, chiefly because of the
dilatory tactics of the French. In the meantime, economic conditions in the three Western zones deteri-
orated. The Soviets tried to squeeze the Western allies
out of Berlin, and climaxed those efforts with their
infamous land blockade of Berlin in June, 1948. They
counteracted the Marshall Plan for Western Europe
with the Mikoyan plan for their own satellite states.
Our foreign policy of rebuilding a free Western Europe including a federal German republic was
strengthened by our decision to stick it out in Berlin
even at the risk of armed conflict and to refuse to negotiate with the Soviet Union on the issue of Germany
until the Soviet blockade of Berlin was lifted. That is
where we stand today.

The results of earlier delay are slowly being overcome; the military governors have come to agreement
with the German parliamentary council in session at
Bonn about the German constitution, and elections for
the federal republic's government could be held this
summer. Since the currency reform in June, 1948, the
economy of Western Germany has recovered remarkably, and conditions in the Trizone are incom-
parably better than those in the Russian zone. According to ECA plans, the foreign trade of Western Germany, inhabited by 50 million people, should reach
balance by 1952.

But it is by no means certain that the federal German republic will be inaugurated. The idea itself is repugnant to the Soviet Union, and the Russians are doing their best to prevent it; they have started negotiations aimed at a new four-power conference on Germany upon lifting the blockade. They hold the important eastern zone of Germany; it contains 17 million Germans and 33 per cent of the four-zonal area. They will not abandon their efforts to eliminate Western influence in Germany and to incorporate the country into their own political orbit.

If any major concession is made to the Soviets on the question of Germany, it will cause the progressive weakening of the structure of Western Europe and undermine the foundations of the Atlantic Pact. Today it is as axiomatic as it ever was that Germany is one of the most essential segments of Western Europe, and that the peace and tranquility of Western Europe depend upon the economic functioning of a free Germany. The Germans are still unquestionably among the most energetic people in Europe, and by history and preference belong to the West. For these very reasons, Germany will remain a key point in American policy toward Europe and Soviet Russia. Keeping a revived Germany on the road to peaceful cooperation requires, first of all, the restoration of fair and equitable relations with a German government composed of men of good will.

Some of the sentences from a memorandum from
Secretary Stimson to Franklin Roosevelt, drafted in
large part by Assistant Secretary of War John J. Mc-
Cloy in September, 1944, contain the arguments pertinent to a constructive policy toward Germany—arguments as valid now as they were then:[5]

"The question is not whether we want Germans to
suffer for their sins. . . . The only question is whether
over the years a group of seventy million educated,
efficient and imaginative people can be kept within
bounds on such a low level of subsistence as the Treasury proposals contemplate. . . . Sound thinking teaches
that . . . poverty in one part of the world usually in-
duces poverty in other parts. Enforced poverty is even
worse, for it destroys the spirit not only of the victim
but debases the victor. It would be just such a crime as
the Germans themselves hoped to perpetrate upon their
victims—it would be a crime against civilization itself.

"This country since its very beginning has maintained
the fundamental belief that all men, in the long run,
have the right to be free human beings and to live in
the pursuit of happiness. Under the Atlantic Charter
victors and vanquished alike are entitled to freedom
from economic want."

---

[5] Henry L. Stimson and McGeorge Bundy, *On Active Service in
Peace and War* (Harper and Brothers, New York, 1948), p. 578.

II.
THE RECONSTRUCTION
OF GERMANY

THE RECONSTRUCTION OF GERMANY

I N this lecture I shall attempt to present a picture of the nature and degree of reconstruction which has actually been accomplished in Germany to date, to discuss the opportunities there are fully to attain the goals of complete recovery, and to set forth the problems which will demand the greatest effort for their solution so as to secure the reconstruction now under way.

When one looks back upon the four years that followed the macabre finale of the Thousand-Year Reich, marked by the suicide of the madman in the Fuehrer bunker, one finds that just the record of four-power decisions made, administrative orders issued, and changes in policy, personnel, and headquarters effected during that period would fill a good-sized library to capacity. Disunity among the Allies, drift and confusion of policy and constant change in Allied personnel constitute one reason for the exhaustively bulky record; but for the most part, the record's size and scope reflect the sweep and complexity of the undertaking itself.

Six years of war, ending in the unconditional surrender of what was once the Wehrmacht, revealed amidst the smoking ruins of German cities a shambles that at one time had been one of the three leading in-

dustrial countries in the world. Not only had massed
bomber assaults destroyed 70 of its major cities and
hundreds of thousands of dwellings, factories, railroad
yards, power plants, and postal and telephone installations. Upon orders of Hitler to leave a deluge behind,
the German SS, in a senseless craze of destruction, had
blown up more than 10,000 bridges, many of them
representing investments of millions of dollars. National, provincial, and local government had ceased to
exist chiefly by virtue of unconditional surrender and
the removal of authority from Nazi officials. The banks
were closed. In Berlin and in the Russian zone the Red
Army cracked open and looted bank vaults and made
off with currency holdings. The whole country
swarmed with released slave workers from many
countries, who "requisitioned" food and other needs
and exacted personal revenge for their plight. Hundreds of thousands of displaced German families and
released soldiers moved about in all directions.

The military governors had to create some order
out of this chaos. It was hoped, and machinery to that
end provided, that despite the country's division into
four zones of occupation, the occupying powers
would instruct their military governors to coordinate
policies and treat the four zones as one economic unit.
However, no joint instructions were ever issued. The
Soviet zone commander, upon orders from Moscow,
disregarded from the outset any intentions the other

zone commanders had. In the Western zones, the policies were parallel in character, but policies in the French zone differed sharply from those in the other two, and many differences existed between British and American policies as well.

During the past four years, the Russian zone has been handled more and more like a Soviet protectorate, until today it is completely separated from the Western zones. Whatever meager reconstruction has taken place there has led to the sovietization of economic, political, and social structures. The large Russian occupation army lives off the land, in contrast to the armies in the other zones, which are supported by their respective home resources. The railroad system in the Russian zone has been reduced to single-track operation. The engines and installations of the electrified system in Saxony have been removed. All the important heavy-industry plants, and the optical, machinery, electrical goods, and china producing factories either have been dismantled and removed as reparations, or have become Soviet property. In so far as the plants do operate, a major part of the output is exported for Soviet account and the proceeds taken as reparations from current production—in violation of the Moscow and Potsdam agreements about reparations.

The buildings on the large estates have been torn down, the farms have been stripped of large-scale equipment, and owners or managers have been driven away or killed. The land itself has been distributed in very small parcels to farm workers and peasants. These activities are classified as the "agrarian reform." The food output of the zone is sharply down; so is industrial production. A new currency has been introduced in the Russian zone—the Ostmark—so far depreciated in its purchasing power that 4 Ostmarks are worth about 1 Westmark at the present time.

Politically, the Russian zone is under the absolute dictate of the SED or Socialist Unity Party, which is the communist party directed by remote control from Moscow. The MVD—uniformed political state police—controls the Russian army living in the zone and the German population of the area. The Russians have also set up a militarized German police organization, under German officers, which is being trained gradually to exercise the same functions as the MVD, and to become a defense force on which the Russians can rely. The military core of this "police force" is made up of about 50,000 persons armed with heavy ordnance; 200,000 additional personnel are equipped only with light weapons.

The Russian zone is unlike anything that could be called Germany or Western Europe today; the proletarianized and sovietized people who live under this foreign tyranny still speak German, and want to be delivered from this police state in which the concentration camps, once filled with victims of the Gestapo again overflow, and in which people are drafted right and left for forced labor in Germany or Russia.

Deep inside the Russian zone lies Berlin, Germany's former capital. Once it had 4.5 million inhabitants; now it has about 3.5 million. The city itself is the largest and most depressing field of ruins to be found anywhere on the Continent. The rubble has been removed from the streets, the water, power, and sewage systems have been repaired, and a portion of the transportation system has been mended to render a primitive sort of service; but no effort at real reconstruction is visible. Due to the disastrous shortage of fuel in spite of brown coal mines nearby, the city's trees have disappeared and the forests in the neighborhood have been chopped down. During the course of the blockade of Berlin, and in retaliation for the airlift, the Soviet commandant cut off the Western sectors of the city from the Russian sector by denying them electric power or other supplies. The Western allies have established a West-German currency in their sectors and have outlawed the Ostmark.

The airlift is one of the greatest technical achievements in mass transportation known in history. In terms of military experience, its cost is recovered many times over, and it has been a first-rate political investment. It has thwarted the attempt to squeeze the Western powers out of Berlin, but the privations of the

2.8 million people living in the Western sectors are beyond description. Yet in spite of that, the Berliners are in good spirits, have unlimited courage, and are determined to stick it out with the Western allies. So long as the 1,000 airlift planes take off and land at the rate of one every minute and a half on three different airfields in the city, every hour of the day and night, the sound of freedom echoes deep inside the Soviet zone.

The signs of visible reconstruction so far achieved are confined to the three Western zones. In fact, because of the rift between the East and the West, the trizonal area is all that can be called "Germany" at the present time. This area of 96,000 square miles (equal to the area of Oregon) harbors today a population of about 48 million (equal to the population of the states of New York, New Jersey, Pennsylvania, Ohio, Indiana, Illinois, and Iowa). It is estimated that by 1952 the number will have risen to 50 million, not counting the inhabitants of the Western sectors of Berlin. About 12 million of these 48 million people are pauperized expellees from areas transferred to Poland, and from Hungary and Czechoslovakia, and a small segment of refugees from the Russian zone. The British zone has received the largest number of expellees and refugees, followed by the American zone, while the French zone has received only an insignificant number.

Western Germany thus has 66 per cent of the whole

prewar German population within its boundaries, a ratio which may rise to 72 per cent by 1952. It contains no more than 59 per cent of Germany's prewar industrial resources, and only 45 per cent of its arable land. With reference to area, population, arable land, food deficit, and need to export industrial goods, Western Germany is today a replica of Great Britain.

It is obvious that the reconstruction of Germany would have been an enormous undertaking in any case. Twelve years of consumptive tyranny, six years of devastating war ending in complete catastrophe, and the loss of six million able-bodied men in the most productive age groups would have demanded compensation in the form of decades of hard work, frugal living, and prudent investment of all savings if the nation was to be brought out of its misery—even without loss of territory and the imposition of additional burdens by the victors. But the problem of reconstruction has been made next to insoluble by the expulsion of 9 million people from a fourth of the land area into the western portion of the country, the dumping of several million other expellees from other countries into that portion, and by the separation of the Russian zone from the West.

Late in 1946 the American and British zones of occupation were consolidated. Early in 1948 the Bizone and the French zone were merged. Unification of the zones was achieved by continuous pressure to that end on the part of the United States. The price we paid for it consisted in our shouldering of the financial burden of the occupation costs for the French and British zones, in as much as they had to be financed by the occupying powers. By virtue of our ERP aid, the largest share of which goes to Britain, followed by France, and by financing the foreign-trade deficit of all three Western zones, our policy has prevailed, although the treatment of Western Germany still is and will continue to be a matter of compromise between the three governments. Unification was marred by the unilateral French action of cutting off the Saar from the Trizone by a customs boundary.

American policy toward the reconstruction of Germany has followed the line described by the Secretary of State in his statement of December 12, 1945, in its central core. At that time he envisaged three tentative stages of recovery. The first, covering 1945 and 1946 was to be concerned primarily with emergency reconstruction and corrective measures. The second, from 1946 to 1948 was to accomplish chiefly the dismantling of industries and the delivery of reparations, and to effect the changes enforced by the occupying powers, but it was also to be a period that would witness some increase in production. The third stage, to begin in 1948, was one in which the Germans were to assume responsibility for their economy, expand production and foreign trade, raise living standards to the

European average, and to become independent of foreign financial aid.

It may be said in retrospect that the anticipated sequence and timing in that calendar has worked out as expected, although matters that were to be characteristic of the first phase unfortunately were all too prevalent in the second, and some corrective measures still hang on in the third. On the other hand, real reconstruction, expected during the third stage of recovery, set in with a more dramatic and sudden force and quickly gained more momentum than had been anticipated.

What diplomatic language calls "corrective measures" included three different types of action: economic disarmament, reparations, and restitution. The visible effect of all three has been the destruction or removal of industrial buildings and their equipment.

According to the Yalta and Potsdam agreements, Germany was to be completely demilitarized. Within a single year of occupation every military establishment and every physical military potential were demolished. Economic disarmament provided for the destruction or removal of those industrial plants useful only for war and for the reduction in numbers—that is, dismantling and removal—of factories useful for peacetime purposes but essential for war, and also provided for control of the output of the remaining factories in that latter category.

The economic disarmament of peace industries with a potential war use was a most controversial issue from the outset. In this age of total warfare, there is scarcely a part of a country's economy which, in the event of war, does not lend itself to conversion for war purposes or does not serve the war effort. If security against the aggressive military adventures of such a country is to be created by removing or keeping under restrictive control essential parts of the economic war potential, such a policy is bound to cripple the normal peacetime economy. That, in turn, requires policing the people and keeping them under the victor's bayonet for as long as the policy is to be kept in force. It makes such a country, even if it were to have a perfectly peaceful government, and were a good neighbor in the family of nations, incapable of defending itself against aggression. Hence such a country requires protection by the defense systems of neighboring nations.

Under the policy of economic disarmament, which the United States intended to pursue as long as circumstances required, 742 major industrial plants in the Western zones were earmarked for removal as excess capacity. In general, Germany's 1936 economic structure was taken as the base for further reductions, although 10 million more people than in 1936 would have to live in the Western zones. Industries manufacturing machine tools and motor cars were to be

reduced to between 10 and 15 per cent; those manufacturing steel and heavy mechanical equipment to 30
per cent; and those producing basic chemicals—which
means chiefly fertilizer—to 50 per cent of 1936 capacity. The production of sea-going vessels, synthetic
nitrogen fertilizer, synthetic rubber and gasoline, ball
and roller bearings, aircraft, and many other things
was strictly prohibited. Only small tractors could be
made, and at the rate of 5,000 a year, although Germany had attained a farm-tractor fleet of 140,000 and
needed about 20,000 tractors a year for replacement
alone. Since tractor plants can in wartime be con-
verted to tank production, even their dismantling was
contemplated. (In the Russian zone, Europe's greatest plow factory was dismantled because during the
war it had made armor plate instead of plowshares and
moldboards.)

The dismantled plants were designed to supply the
bulk of reparations to 18 nations. While the Russians
were supposed to satisfy their reparations demands
from their own zone, they were also to receive 25 per
cent of all capital assets taken from the three Western
zones. An additional form of reparations concerned
all patent rights, which were summarily expropriated
and thrown open to the world. Economic disarmament also involved a thorough investigation of all scientific research, public and private, and all current and
projected work of inventors and designers. Following

this screening of the vanquished nation's productive brains, hundreds of top scientists and engineers were invited and otherwise induced to continue their work in the countries of the victors.

Restitution added another claim upon existing German industrial capacity and equipment of unknown proportions. It was logical and just that such equipment, as well as other assets requisitioned or looted by the Nazi regime in other countries or taken from the German victims of the regime be restored to the original owners. In practice, the restitution clause opened the gates to a flood of claims having nothing to do with the intended purpose. Machines, trucks, and other costly equipment purchased before the war by German companies from Czech, French, and other producers were claimed on the basis of restitution. So were German machines which during Allied bombing raids had been temporarily stored in areas later annexed by the victors.

In reality, a large number of the measures resulting in de-industrialization and extreme restrictions to be forced upon vital German industries were ultimately not carried out, simply because the effects of such measures proved to be too destructive for other nations and promised to make the whole problem of restoring some foundation for living to the German people completely impossible to solve. The original plan of March, 1946, designated 742 industrial plants for dismantling on the assumption that the four zones would be treated and would function as an economic unit. When it became evident that this assumption could not be entertained, and that a far greater industrial capacity would be needed to compensate, through larger industrial exports, for the increased food deficit caused by separation from the arable land of the Russian zone, the level of industries was revised upward, and the dismantling program was halted temporarily for review. The food deficit was doubled by the greater population density in the Western zones, which further underscored the need for a greater industrial capacity there to earn the foreign exchange to purchase food imports.

The Potsdam agreement declared that the removal of industrial plants was to be finished by March, 1948, but in the autumn of 1948 about 680 plants marked for dismantling were still on the list and the subject of conference. Protests from many sides in the United States were made against the whole dismantling program, which by now was overlapping into the third phase of occupation, that of reconstruction. Herbert Hoover, sent by President Truman to Germany in 1947 to give counsel on the economic situation and to suggest remedies, strongly recommended the abandonment of the dismantling program. In the foreword to a pamphlet entitled *Destruction at Our Expense,* he said in part:[6]

---

[8] Christopher Emmet and Fritz Baade, *Destruction at Our Expense* (New York, 1947), p. 1.

At a time when the world is crying, and even dying, from lack of industrial production we apparently pursue the policy of destruction of the gigantic productive equipment in the Western zones of Germany. It means less essential goods to all Europe, greater delay in recovery of the world and larger drains on the American taxpayer.

The Herter Committee report, the Krug report, the Harriman report, and comprehensive studies by leading industrialists like Lewis Brown also recommended that dismantling be stopped and the whole economic treatment of Germany changed. Yet it was not until 1949 that the Humphrey committee recommended the removal of 167 plants from the list, and that the Western allies accepted the recommendation. Unfortunately, 8 of these 167 plants recommended for retention were again marked for dismantling, and these 8 represent two-thirds of the value of the 167, and comprise some vital links in the industrial process. Thus, late in April, 1949, dismantling begins anew.

During the first three years of the occupation, reconstruction consisted of restoring the food-rationing system, getting agricultural production on its feet by securing fertilizer, seed, and spare parts for implements. It was a continual struggle to make any headway. The food deficit was covered from abroad, mainly from the United States. While strong efforts were made to boost production in Germany, the goal of 1,550 calories a day for normal consumers was far

below what was necessary to maintain work efficiency.
Three times in succession the food-rationing system
broke down. In the early, months of 1946, 1947, and
1948 rations fell to disastrously low levels. In May,
1947, food riots broke out and a general strike and
bloodshed were avoided only by an emergency ship-
ment of 70 vessels loaded with flour and grain. Early
in 1946 the American army intended to raise the rations in our zone to 2,000 calories daily, but for various
reasons did not even obtain the necessary allocations
or appropriations for maintaining the 1,500-calorie ration. For three years the food situation remained the
Number One economic issue in the Western zones. It
overshadowed everything else. Health deteriorioated,
and people lost more and more weight. Labor was
listless and ineffective. Scarcities led to an ever-grow-
ing black market in food, on which supplies were small
and prices exorbitant. At length, food could be traded
on the black market only for scarce goods. Coal
miners had to be induced with food packages to increase their output. A disastrous drought in 1947 and
a subsequently severe winter made the situation even
more acute. The food shortage was worst in the
French zone, where a large occupation force lived off
the land; in the Bizone the occupation forces did not
use any German-grown food.

In other respects, however, economic recovery
made some modest though important progress during

the first three years of occupation. The 12 million expellees and refugees were assigned emergency quarters
on farms, and in villages and towns. Railroads were
repaired and resumed operation. In all the cities sani-
tation was set in order and streets and passages were
cleared of debris and rubble. The coal mines were
manned and re-opened. Gradually, postal and telephone services were restored. Late in 1946 some cot-
ton, and later some hides and wool, began to be imported to start up the textile and tanning industries.
The export trade began to function. Exports consisted
chiefly of lumber, coal, and scrap iron. In the French
zone, the world-famous Black Forest was subjected to
drastic cutting for export, thus depleting this natural
resource for decades to come. Forests in the British
zone were similarly depleted. Since most of the Ruhr
coal output was allocated to other countries, wood had
to be used as fuel for houses. The domestic shortage
of coal frustrated the industries producing building
materials such as glass, roof tiles, brick, cement, and
iron goods. Hundreds of factories could not begin
operating because the decision had not yet been made
to permit them to operate.

German industries had been highly integrated and
organized with many vertical trusts and combines as
well as cartels before the war. Point 12 of the Potsdam agreement stipulated that the German economy
was to be decentralized for the purpose of eliminating

the excessive concentration of economic power exemplified particularly by cartels, syndicates, trusts, and other monopolistic arrangements. While in the Soviet zone Soviet-owned trusts were created and a maximum centralization of economic power was built up by central industrial commissariats, in the Bizone the procedure was exactly the opposite. At the same time it wavered and was not fully coordinated in the British and American areas. In executing the policy bewildering problems were encountered. A British report stated that the efforts toward complete decartellization had created chaos in the Ruhr. All of this set back real reconstruction. Decartellization was carried out in the French zone, but there whole industries were subject to central control by French agencies which became merely French-controlled cartels. The French, in conjunction with that program, using the threat of dismantling and other pressures, induced German owners of industries to sell the majority of their shares to French groups.

Other delays in recovery were caused by the effects of Allied political policies. The Potsdam protocol provided that all active members of the Nazi party be removed from public and semi-public office and from positions of responsibility in important private undertakings. This "denazification" policy of screening, classifying, vindicating, or convicting the whole population for its political views and acts over a period of twelve

years was an enormous, most involved, and dubious
enterprise which was carried out for several years.
Aside from the questionable political wisdom of the
procedure chosen, it had the effect of preventing a
large part of the remaining managerial talent in industry and in the administration of economic affairs
from going to work.

The very worst obstacle to recovery—an obstacle
that overshadowed all others, including even the
prominent shortage of food, was the inflation of the
currency and its constantly diminishing purchasing
power. The supply of currency in Western Germany
alone amounted to almost 150 billion Reichsmarks.
Wages, only slightly higher than at the war's end,
were virtually frozen, and prices for rationed goods
were controlled. The supply of goods through normal
channels decreased continually, and the black markets
indicated the real purchasing power of the former currency—it had already reached the point of being re-
jected as payment for scarce goods. This situation
gradually paralyzed the whole economic system. Railroads and highways were jammed with people scurry-
ing after food, which they obtained by swapping for
it whatever goods they still possessed. Thousands of
people remained idle because they could no longer
afford to work for a paper wage with which they
could not buy anything except the meagre food ration.
A pair of soles for their shoes, available only in the

black market, cost more than a month's wages. Factories could not keep their workers unless they supplied them with at least one substantial meal a day without ration coupons. The factories got the food for these meals by making arrangements with farmers and fisheries whereby produce was exchanged for industrial goods withheld from legal channels of trade. This was known as the "grey" market—a semi-legal enterprise that was unlawful but was not prosecuted. Yet all these illegal detours around a regimented economy that had lost control of the situation and the respect of those under its jurisdiction took a great deal of time and energy; and it amounted to wasted effort—the greatest waste of all consisting of the vast bureaucracy that ran the ineffective controls.

This sad process finally brought the whole economy virtually to a standstill during the first five months of 1948, and the people to the brink of desperation. Stores had no more goods to sell, and the cigarette had taken the place of the mark. Just as in 1923, the people were trying to rid themselves of the paper money by exchanging it for any goods representing a real value, thus forcing the issue of currency reform.

All this was finished by one stroke, as if by magic. On June 20, 1948, the old currency was outlawed and a new one, issued on the basis of $6\frac{1}{2}$ Deutsche Mark for 100 Reichsmark, or at a rate of 1 to 16. Six months later the total circulation, including new credits and bank deposits, amounted to 16 billion Deutsche Mark. The new currency is confined to the German market and does not have an official exchange rate. For purposes of foreign trade, the conversion factor has been fixed at $.30 (U.S.) per Deutsche Mark.

Of all the actions taken by the Western allies, the currency reform has been the most effective measure looking toward the reconstruction of the German economy. It was long overdue. Had it been taken earlier, a rise in production and a spiritual uplift for the German population would have been achieved earlier. This action was postponed so long because it was felt desirable to prevent a break with the Russians in the Allied Control Council. The price we paid for the currency reform was the blockade of Berlin. In view of the Soviets' flagrant violation of all their commitments in the occupation of Germany and the exhaustion of the last vestige of a chance to arrive at a basis for agreement or cooperation, the currency reform was necessary and airlift was not too high a price to pay for the step taken. This was the more true since the issue at stake between the Soviets and the three Western occupation powers concerned no specific action taken in Germany. The issue was the whole political contest between the Soviets and the West over the reconstruction of Western Europe, involving also violation of agreements concerning Poland, Hungary, and Czechoslovakia and a great many other manifestations of Soviet global strategy.

The currency reform was accompanied by several other measures. Our government made $2 billion available to the West-German economy for the year 1948, providing means for importing enough food to improve the basic German ration to 1,850 calories, as well as enough fertilizer, petroleum, and gasoline and textile raw materials to prime the pipelines of production. This energetic policy of starting real industrial recovery was postponed for so long a time because the United States had to straighten out her differences with Great Britain; and when that was accomplished at the price of shouldering the full financial burden of the British zone, the tenacious opposition of the French to the revival of the Ruhr steel industries had to be overcome. For a long while the French resistance was more effective than that of the Russians.[7] In conjunction with strong financial aid from America and the currency reform, a further lift to the West German economy was given when the German bizonal economic administration freed large parts of the economy, except food, textiles, and shoes, from price control and rationing, after ten years of the strictest regimentation. Since a bumper crop had begun to be harvested, all truck crops and potatoes were also de-rationed.

Wages and the prices of rationed items remained the same under the new currency as they had been under

---

[7] Cf. Demaree Bess, "Our Chilly War with France," *Saturday Evening Post*, May 21, 1949.

the old mark. But all the savings and capital funds in public and private hands were practically wiped out. Only in cases where owners had succeeded in converting their Reichsmarks into stores of goods was any capital retained.

The combined currency reform and restoration of a competitive market economy and free enterprise had a most astonishing effect. Within a few days, people who had not been working or who had exhausted their energy on long trips in search for a few potatoes eagerly looked for jobs. Farmers began feverishly to harvest vegetables and early potatoes. The markets soon were swamped with this produce, and the prices gave way. Railroad stations became deserted, because people could no longer afford to travel. Shops displayed supplies of all sorts of goods of fine quality and at relatively low prices. In a few weeks, enough of the new money was in circulation via wages and sales to start consumer purchases to replenish pantries, kitchens, and homes with the essentials of daily life. Until then, matches, pottery, kitchen hardware, light globes, paper, pencils, and shoe laces had been unobtainable.

The supply of hardware, glass, and china proved to be sufficient to stop the buying rush. Their prices rose slightly. Textiles, shoes, and other leather goods remained in short supply and prices rose substantially. This held true until shortly before Christmas, and the public grew nervous about inflationary tendencies and the visible loss of purchasing power. The labor unions called a protest strike for one day. But no suggestion was made that price controls be restored, because everyone knew only too well that prices would be fixed according to consumer desire but that goods again would disappear. Nobody wanted to return to economic methods that belonged to and required the totalitarian state and its police despotism.

Prompt and intelligent action by the German chief of the bizonal economic administration, Professor Ludwig Erhard, saved the situation. This action was in part prepared by the large council of economic advisers, representing all shades of economic opinion yet advising on specific courses of action. Mr. Erhard persuaded the banks to tighten the supply of credit and initiated an interim program to supply the market with low-priced consumer goods of average quality. This so-called Jedermann Program (Everyman's Program) involved a voluntary agreement among industrial producers to process certain quotas of raw materials into the desired category of goods and to put them on sale at specified prices. At the same time, large stocks of surplus army textiles and shoes were imported from the United States and put on the market. This stopped the consumer buying rush and prices began to decline. These tendencies have gained momentum in recent months. In fact, coupons are only nominally in use. Production in the bizone has jumped sharply since June 20, 1948. The output of Ruhr coal, which was 255,000 tons daily in January, 1948, rose to 330,000 tons in January, 1949. The index of industrial production (1936 equalling 100) rose from 51 in June, 1948, to 78 in December, and will probably reach 90 by June, 1949.

All these data simply indicate what you can see with your own eyes in the Anglo-American zone, and to a much smaller extent in the French zone—namely, after three years of slow motion and despair, we have finally undertaken the real job and have succeeded in getting reconstruction under way in Germany. The food is still poor in quality and composition, but people no longer go hungry all the time, and they are regaining weight. They have lost the fear of starving to death, and have abandoned the nightmare that the victors were pursuing a hideous plan to destroy them by controlled starvation. They have new hope, because they see that their exertion and dogged work hold out some promise that over a period of several decades their devastated country can be rebuilt. Reconstruction has succeeded against all the terrible odds because the German people have intelligently cooperated with the military government in the three zones, and, in all their misery, have kept their chins up and have worked harder than any people I have ever seen work anywhere in the world.

All of this is most encouraging. Only the merchants of hate and the preachers of vengeance will view with misgiving this ray of hope in a people whom the Lord has punished as severely as any nation on earth was ever punished. Politically, this ray of hope is one of our greatest assets in the effort to keep Western Europe out of the claws of communism and Soviet tyranny. Recovery in Western Germany still lags far behind the recovery that has taken place elsewhere in Western Europe. Yet it has reached a point where, by comparison with living conditions in the Russian zone, the situation is so favorably viewed that the people living in that zone, including the German communists, regard the West as a land where democracy works. The clandestine migration under the Iron Curtain moves west, not east.

To an economist this life-sized experiment of reviving the economy of the most powerful industrial country in Europe after its total collapse is most fascinating. What interests him most, however, is the question whether the goal of the reconstruction is attainable or not. So far some progress has been made, but it is the American taxpayer who is keeping the German people alive. Will it be possible to boost production in Western Germany high enough so that it may earn enough by exports to pay for the necessary imports of food, raw materials, and industrial goods? West-German agriculture will not be able to produce more than 60 per cent of the food needed, even if it is further intensified and the people have a more frugal diet than they formerly enjoyed. In order to restore consumption to a level of 85 per cent of 1936, exports must be boosted to nearly $3 billion a year. Exports are expected to reach a total of about 20 per cent of that sum for 1948-49. If that increase is to be accomplished, many changes must be made. The economy must expand its effective capacity. More electric power and generating capacity are needed. Housing conditions must be improved, and transport facilities expanded. Coal and steel production must be increased, and the share of coal and lumber going into export channels must be reduced from their present 50 per cent level to one of 15 per cent, manufactured goods to take their place as exports.

To accomplish all this, the German economy needs large amounts of investment capital, and that capital can be derived only from domestic savings or from foreign investment. Foreign investment is at present impossible because investors are neither permitted to invest nor do they have security for capital or permission to transfer interest and dividends. So long as the future of Germany and with it the future of Western Europe hang so precariously in the balance from one power conference to the next, investment capital will not flow into Europe and particularly not into Germany. Hence, if the German economy is to "sweat out" capital in the form of domestic savings at a rate approaching investment needs, total productivity must rise far above what it is today, so that the German wage earner will have an opportunity to save and still to consume on a level that will not undermine his health or his incentive to work.

German trade must flow freely into the world, including the United States. This will be impossible if foreign countries, or rather, small groups in foreign countries boycott German goods or even go so far as to doom to failure and force the closing of a small-scale export exhibit put on by the Western allied military governments, which occurred a few days ago in New York. It is obvious that such actions as those to prohibit German artists from earning foreign exchange for the German economy, and that of arbitrarily preventing German foreign trade from even displaying its goods, clearly sabotage the carefully considered policy of the United States, Great Britain, and France concerning the reconstruction of a peaceful Germany for the benefit of all Western Europe. It is also obvious that a shameful state of affairs exists when an insignificantly small minority, motivated by negative if understandable emotions, is permitted further to increase the damage wrought by the Morgenthau Plan, a scheme which was properly called an attempted crime against humanity. Reference has already been made to the fact that with respect to its economic geography, Western Germany is the replica of Great Britain. If Britain, a victorious power, and with the aid of the United States, the Commonwealth, her merchant marine, and her freedom of restrictions on industrial development and trade has a hard time getting enough foreign exchange, it is evident how much more of a venture it must be for the German people to export enough to survive.

The difficulty in the way of the task of obtaining, with continued ECA support, the required increase in production and exports can be seen not only from the cautious and warning reports of the ECA administrator, but also from the recent action taken by the council of foreign ministers of the United States, Great Britain, and France to lift some of the restrictions imposed on German industries. The building of seagoing vessels up to 7,000 tons with a speed not in excess of 12 knots is now permitted, as is the production of ball bearings, aluminum, heavy tractors, and nitrogen fertilizer. It may be assumed that in due time some further relaxation of the corrective measures will be granted in order to secure the success of the recovery and indirectly to assist the whole Atlantic community.

What has been said up to now about the economic reconstruction of Germany of course leaves open the most pertinent question of all. To what extent has there been progress in political and social reconstruction, and will its ultimate success establish guarantees against new threats of military adventure? The whole course of Allied efforts in this respect is at least as involved as the record of four years of economic reconstruction, of which some selected highlights were discussed. It exceeds the limits of this lecture to attempt even an outline of this course. All that can be done is to show some of the contours of the new political features already visible.

Today the Trizone is politically organized into nine separate states and two free cities with state rank, making a total of 11 states. Each has its own parliament and its elected democratic government. The political parties have been reorganized; the Nazi party has been outlawed; any sort of royalist party has been excluded; and the communist party has been admitted to political participation. The Christian-Democratic Union (CDU) and the Social Democratic Party (SPD) have more than 80 per cent of the votes, the CDU at present being stronger than the SPD. In addition to these two, there is a liberal democratic party on the extreme left and a few splinter parties holding a few per cent of the votes. The main difference between the two leading parties concerns the degree of state control and planning in business and the degree of centralization a federal government should have. The CDU stands for a minimum of government controls, for free enterprise, and for as little central power as is unavoidable. The SPD sponsors the nationalization of a sector of key industries and a certain amount of planned economy in addition to free enterprise, and hence advocates strong central power for the federal government. The communists, controlling some 5 per cent of the votes, follow the Moscow line, pick on the mistakes of the military governments, and fight along the line of militant nationalism.

Upon the initiative of the three Western occupying powers a German parliamentary council at Bonn has worked out a constitution for a West-German federal republic which was recently approved by the three powers, who in turn have agreed upon an occupation statute which delimits their functions, rights, and obligations after the German republic has been created. According to this statute the occupying powers will retain decisions on currency, investment, allocation of basic research resources, foreign policy, and on foreign trade. The date for the inauguration of the German state is near at hand. Military governors are supposed to be succeeded by three high commissioners working under the foreign ministers rather than under the armies. The occupation of the demilitarized republic will be confined more and more to policing and military security service. Once this republic becomes a fact, a part of what the policy of unconditional surrender destroyed will have been repaired.

All of this moves in the direction of German resumption of responsibility for their own domestic affairs. The new state will still be a torso and will be deprived of all the elements essential to sovereignty. It will not include the 17 million Germans in the Russian

zone or the 2.8 million people in the Western sectors
of Berlin. But still, it will be a major step toward fill-
ing the political and economic vacuum created by the
destruction of Germany, and in a manner that prevents
Russia from simply taking over and making all of
Western Europe untenable. Moreover, the ground is
being prepared for the integration of this new German
state into the fabric of a cooperating Western Europe,
as a member of the Atlantic community.

On the basis of their general course of expansion and
autarchic imperialism, it is only logical that the Soviets
will continue to do everything in their power to prevent the formation of the West-German republic.
Now they are offering to lift the blockade in exchange
for a promise from the West to refer the whole problem of Germany to a new four-power conference. It
stands to reason that such an offer should be accepted
if there is certainty that no further conditions are
added. But to maintain our freedom of action, we
should by all means keep the airlift in full operation
after we have lifted our counterblockade and the rail-
way lines and the autobahn to Berlin have been re-
opened, and until such time as a genuine new agreement has been reached in four-power negotiations. If
the airlift were abandoned, and if the new negotiations
should end as all the previous meetings have ended, it
would be most difficult to restore the airbridge to
Berlin.

There is every reason to be firm and uncompromising in our determination to incorporate a democratic Germany into a stronger, cooperative Western Europe. If Germany had been treated as an economic unit begining in March, 1946, economic reconstruction would have made much headway, and the American taxpayer would have been saved a great deal of money. But invoking the Potsdam formula at the present time would upset all the reconstruction efforts so far made in the West, and would inevitably require more financial assistance from the outside than ever. The Russian zone is a vacuum, milked dry by Soviet policies; the union of this zone with Trizonia would initiate a heavy flow of capital goods and raw materials from the West into this gaping hole. Since a large part of the industrial production of the Russian zone is exported for Soviet account, it is probable that under unification with the Western zones, the Soviets could drain a substantial amount of the goods flowing from those zones into their own treasury. Thus, in effect, the American taxpayer, who is providing the funds to restore the Western zones, would be paying reparations to Russia.

The whole political and administrative organization of the Russian zone is just as incompatible with what has laboriously been built up in the Trizone as is the economic climate. In the Western zones, democratic institutions and law prevail. Union with the Russian zone at present would simply turn Russia's agents loose again on the Western zones to strengthen the communist party.

It does not seem probable that these immense obstacles to a real understanding between the four powers on the German issue, to say nothing of the conflict on nearly all the world's diplomatic fronts, can easily or quickly be overcome. If we do not want to jeopardize all that we have won by our determined Marshall Plan aid, we must go through with the inauguration of the West-German republic and its integration into Western Europe. This does not mean that the unification of all of Germany is unnecessary; on the contrary, it is necessary, but it would be folly to try it at the moment. After the West-German republic has been set up, it will need a period of 18 months or two years before it becomes a going concern internally consolidated. After that, and with proper international safeguards, a merger with the Soviet zone could be negotiated under far more favorable auspices.

At the present time, an interim solution for normal trade relations between the Western zones and the Soviet zone, together with a modus vivendi for the four powers in Berlin, should be worked out. A trade and communications agreement between East and West and for Berlin, an official exchange rate between D Mark and Ost Mark, and exchange facilities, seem to be all that is necessary for a year or two.

The establishment of a West-German republic raises another question. Have the German people learned enough from the total disaster they experienced following the suffering they brought to other nations? On all sides in America, people ask whether the Germans have really begun to understand democracy, and whether or not we can trust them.

So far as we can now discern, there is no reason for pessimism or cynicism on this score. Under our guidance and with our aid the Germans have revived a free press, are making use of their freedom of speech and assembly, vote with good judgment, and are reforming their educational system. With reference to the great issue of our time—freedom versus serfdom under totalitarianism—they have made the right choice in the midst of the greatest privation. The amazing truth is that in the greatest fields of ruins on the whole continent of Europe, the hungry and destitute German people did not vote communist, but instead laid the foundations for a genuine democracy and elected leaders of well-known and well-tested democratic convictions, many of whom stood up under Gestapo torture in the days of the tyranny.

It may be said that we have indeed made a good start toward the economic reconstruction of Western Germany, and to some moderate extent also in the direction of the political restoration of a West-German state. Yet there still remains a great deal to do before

we can say that full and final success has been a-
chieved. Upon that ultimate victory depends not only
the definitive recovery of Europe, but the answer to
the greatest question of our day—will we have another, more devastating war soon, or may we instead
look forward to eventual peace?

III.
THE INTEGRATION OF GERMANY
INTO WESTERN EUROPE

THE INTEGRATION OF GERMANY
INTO WESTERN EUROPE

It has been the historical achievement of the American people under the leadership of Franklin Roosevelt that they delivered Europe from tyranny at the cost of precious blood and enormous wealth. Yet, under this great leader, those very sacrifices gave aid to tyranny in another shape; and inept diplomacy surrendered more than half of Europe and most of China and Korea to it. If America had been more prudent in foreign affairs, and if our diplomacy more daring while our soldiers were winning battles in the face of terrible adversity all over the world, the political fruits of victory would not have unwittingly been given away. The tragedy is that American sacrifices thus should have cast a dark shadow upon the destiny of any freedom-loving people. In the years following, the nation has come to recognize some of the worst blunders. We have changed the direction of our foreign policy, and we have abandoned Roosevelt's "great design" of building world government and world peace on friendship with the Soviet government. And we have begun to fight for the preservation of freedom and human rights in the parts of the world where those values have not yet been blotted out by the expanding Soviet tyranny.

We suffered further serious loss through the absorption of Czechoslovakia into the Soviet orbit of power and the progressive erosion of the remnants of free China. But we may count some gains, too. We successfully defended the Greeks, we strengthened Turkey; energetic ECA assistance diverted the tide of communism in Italy and France, and we took a strong stand on behalf of the reconstruction of a free and democratic Germany. In the defense of that greatly shrunken part of Europe lying west of the Iron Curtain, a reconstructed Germany is a primary bastion. The western boundary of the Russian occupation zone in Germany today sharply divides the world of the omnipotent police state reaching from Vladivostok to Helmstedt and Coburg and the Western world of freedom and human rights. If the people and the land of Western Germany had suddenly become subject to Soviet rule as was the fate of Czechoslovakia, it is plain that neither France nor the Lowlands could long have retained their independence.

The force of the relentless diplomatic hammer blows of the Soviet foreign minister, ambassadors, and delegates to the United Nations, together with the supporting demonstrations by the various national leaders of the communist parties, made us realize that the Soviets were making an open bid for all of Germany as well as Italy and France. So we fortified the exposed frontier of Western Europe by changing our policy toward Germany. We won the support of Great Britain and France to the immediate reconstruction of Germany and, shouldering the financial burden it entailed, we began to execute the program. We had three compelling reasons for deciding to rebuild an industrial Germany in close association with Western Europe. If we failed to do it, the Soviets would soon fill the gap and take all of Germany. If, on the other hand, we did rebuild the country, success depended on weaving it economically and politically into the fabric of the West; and, if we wanted to bring recovery in Western Europe to the stage of security and stability, we needed Germany's industrial supplies and coal, and access to her market for Western produce.

Some respectable German leaders of the older generation who hold democratic convictions believe that Germany should regain a neutral position between East and West—tied to neither side but able to play the role of interpreter, mediator, and perhaps conciliator between the two worlds. This idea has the fatal defect of requiring either a strong and powerful Germany which will defend its neutral position, or a Germany kept neutral by agreement among today's great powers. Owing to the tragic course of German history during the last 16 years, the first alternative already belong to the past. In fact, this central doctrine of Bismarck's foreign policy was ignored under the

Kaiser. The other alternative, that of neutralizing Germany by agreement among the four powers concerned is just as impractical, because it not only presupposes the wisest and most virtuous German leadership, but also because it involves much too great a risk for the Western powers—by infiltration and similar tactics a neutralized Germany might overnight become a satellite Soviet state. Furthermore, it presupposes a blind faith in the possibility of discovering a basic unity of purpose between the West and the Soviets. This unity being conspicuously absent, the diplomatic machinery needed for keeping Germany neutralized would extend the Soviet veto power to every move, economic or otherwise, that the Germans or the Western powers might make with respect to affairs in Western Germany.

So far the case for the attachment of a reconstructed Germany to the West seems plain. However, as soon as we begin to tackle the job of linking Germany with the West and try to translate general policy into specific measures, the really knotty problems begin to emerge. As we shall see, the projected West state as such, even given enough time, far from promises to solve either the German or the West-European issue of foreign affairs.

So long as we focus our efforts chiefly on the economic program by which to balance Germany's foreign trade within another three or four years, and make all the adjustments required to that end, we have the sensation of standing on firm, but most uncomfortable ground. But as soon as we try to come to grips with the idea of integrating Germany into Western Europe, a multitude of perplexing necessities and unpleasant alternatives appears. We are driven to making decisions which themselves presuppose that if we really want to carry them out, we shall have to first change some tenaciously held opinions.

Economic and military considerations provide neither the sole nor the major motivation in our foreign policy. Aside from the consideration of practical defense strategy, it was the political and spiritual essence of Western Europe and the common cultural and religious heritage which made America fight two world wars for their protection. Acting in accord with the same joint motives, we have just committed ourselves to fight a third world war, if need be, in order to secure the freedom and sovereignty of the nations in this area of common culture and heritage, and to guarantee that whatever association among one another they choose be the result of their free and independent decision. Their communal ties with us and our interest in the defense of their freedom as sovereign states are merely the expression of our community of ideals and convictions about the value of respect for individual personality and the nature and purpose of the organized human society. We have concluded a mutual defense pact with the European nations because we want to save our souls by saving these precious values which are threatened by a system of government which in pursuit of materialistic goals and in its expansion of power knows neither respect for human dignity nor goodness to man. This West-European group of nations shares with us the conviction that the Soviet process of subjugating other peoples under puppet governments and reducing them to satellite status amounts to aggression and tyranny. All this makes it impossible to integrate into this group of countries one member which has less than colonial status.

This is particularly impossible if the nation in question happens to be the most populous and the industrially most advanced and productive of them all. The whole idea of the German people's being not just another subsidiary Soviet republic or satellite state, but rather being aligned on the side of the free Western nations makes sense only in so far as it envisages the full restoration of Germany to the status of a free Western nation. In other words, *the integration of Germany into Western Europe requires her restoration economically to a status which will make her independent of subsidies with all possible speed, and even more does it require her prompt political and spiritual restoration as a sovereign and responsible neighbor, now.* Otherwise, the Germans will not fulfill the economic expectations of Western Europe, because a healthy economy presuppposes a society which is politically free and thereby obliged to cope with its own economic and social needs. This is especially true for a people which must deal with such gigantic areas of debris and human tragedy. Without political sovereignty the German people will feel exploited by the conquerors. The able leaders of the well-organized German labor unions are much too advanced to encourage them to work to capacity under a government which has even less autonomy over domestic affairs than a colony. This holds particularly for the coal miners of the Ruhr.

The two preceding lectures tried to show how much progress we have made in changing our policy from "pastoralization" to re-industrialization and the foundation of a federal German republic, and how much actual reconstruction has been accomplished in the Trizone. In our broader policy toward Western Europe, too, we have come a long way from the failure of a world-peace plan via the United Nations to the Truman doctrine, the Marshall Plan, actual reconstruction under the Economic Cooperation Administration, and to collective security through mutual defense under the Atlantic Pact. But the road from the planned inauguration of the West-German state to the integration of Germany into Western Europe is still blocked by most serious political obstacles created

by allied dictate. These stumbling blocks are solidly
fixed in the attitudes that prevail among the victors,
most of all in our own country.

Our attitude toward Germany is still influenced by
emotions hanging on from the era of appeasement and
the war years, by a host of neatly coined prejudices,
half-truths, and popular but ill-considered judgments,
and by confusion on the need for welding Germany
into the fabric of Western Europe *now* lest we lose
her altogether. In democracies, the actual foreign
policy pursued is strongly influenced and limited in its
scope of action by public opinion and sentiment, particularly when the treatment of a chief defeated enemy
country is concerned. If we do not overcome the
psychological obstacles that impede constructive diplomatic moves by making a rational effort to liberate
ourselves from them, it will take many years for us
finally to arrive at the necessary solution, and then it
will be too late. It is clearly predictable that the whole
opportunity for attaining the pacification of the Continent and creating much closer cooperation among the
West-European nations definitely depends on action
now. It is not an opportunity that will remain available for the next ten years. It is even doubtful whether
it will be present two or three years from now. So far
the initiative in the cold war is still held by the Kremlin, which aptly exploits every opportunity created by
the Western powers' too-little-too-late policies.

The psychological obstacles are stronger in our own

country than they are in Europe; yet the European nations were the ones which were conquered and suffered five or six years of occupation by Nazi Germany. Our homeland never felt the blow of a single bomb. Under these circumstances, and contrary to popular assumption, the possibility of reconciliation between the French and the Germans (to mention just one of the more important intra-Continental relations) is much closer now than it was after World War I. Great Britain absorbed frightful blows from the Luftwaffe, the doodlebugs, and the V-2's, yet the British people are far less vindictive in their attitude toward the Germans than are considerable numbers of very articulate American people. Furtwängler can conduct a symphony orchestra in London and receive an appreciative ovation for his artistry. Yet Furtwängler and Walter Gieseking alike, though invited to perform before American audiences, were forced to cancel their engagements.

The United States of America is the world power that will decide the destiny of the West-German state now being shaped under our initiative. The worst obstacles in the far more complex job of integrating Germany into Western Europe are lodged in our mental attitude about Germany, which in turn breed hesitation, indecision, and delay in taking action. It is therefore important to indicate the issues and the views that desperately need re-examination.

The projected West-German state will only amount

to a colonial administration. The vital economic areas
of government—currency, credit, taxation, allocation
of resources, foreign trade, foreign relations, and police power—are all reserved by the Occupation Statute
to occupation-power decision. Military affairs are
naturally the exclusive domain of the occupying
powers and concern the enforcement of complete de-
militarization. The defense of Germany against outside aggression is a wide-open question. The Occupation Statute of the Western powers considerably im-
proves the situation, but even under it the German
people in the West State will be treated as a nation
with a criminal record that has been put on probation.
This condition invalidates any effort to integrate Germany into Western Europe. One cannot integrate into
a society of free sovereign nations a very important
candidate that is under strict tutelage without degrading the whole society of nations involved. Moreover,
one cannot obtain any benefit from restoring confidence in the leaders of the West-German state if such
confidence is granted only bit by bit. Confidence on
the installment plan is a *contradictio in adjecto* and
simply means modified suspicion. What the people in
Germany who shoulder the responsibility for rebuilding the country and cooperating with the West most
need is the full-fledged confidence which they deserve.

Possibly it is extremely hard to realize at a distance
of 9,000 miles what the policy of the four years of

occupation has left in its wake. Let me try to explain a little how much more involved the situation becomes as soon as you enter Germany than would the tenor of most discussions we Americans hold over here ever lead one to believe. Here in America, people want to know: How far have the Germans advanced toward democracy by now? Have we taught them what democracy is? Have they understood that, and are they at last taking the cue from us? The next most popular question here is whether the Germans have admitted guilt and are repenting.

Now, if you go into Germany and meet with German students in seminars or after dinner, or talk with coal miners in their washrooms between shifts, or with farmers, and bring up this whole subject, you discover that all of them are keenly interested in the question of how to build a better society and improve the individual's lot. After all, who could be more interested in that subject than people who have seen cities that stood in Caesar's time crumble into rubble, and who comprise a nation of ruin-dwellers? But in talking to them as an American who takes pride in the airlift and in the reconstruction our military government has ultimately set in motion with the support of billions of dollars, you soon find out that in these discussions you are only in half as good a position as you had supposed. You find that the word "democracy" itself has for German ears as phony a sound as had the shining conceptual mirages with which Goebbels used to fill them. Having undergone 12 years of propaganda, and suffering painfully from having at one time believed some of it, the Germans of today are more skeptical, critical, and less easily impressed than almost any other people. They will ask why, instead of teaching democracy, we don't practice it in occupied countries. They want to know whether democracy is something real that applies to them, too. And they have most serious doubts on that score. In fact, at the Cologne carnival, with a blend of good humor and political satire, the people called themselves the "natives of Trizonesia." Can you blame them for this skepticism? When the gruesome ordeal of being bombed out for years, living in cellars, running for shelter, and dragging the dead out from under the ruins finally came to an end, with the Gestapo and SS terror increasing with each passing day, most of the German people were convinced that the Nazi leaders were insane, and prayed on their knees that American and British troops deliver them from their German tormentors. For several months after the fighting stopped, the German population wanted to accept their conquerors as liberators, and to do everything possible to make up for the criminal deeds of their leaders, the worst of whom had left the scene by suicide. But Western troops had strict orders against fraternization and were told to be tough on the Germans. Indeed, they were still regularly indoctrinated to hate all Germans as a race of paranoiacs who, by their innate militarism, had put themselves under the leadership of war-mongering industrialists and militarists. This had rather appalling effects. The Germans saw that American and British troops did not respect private property in the home. In many cases these incidents and the Jim Crow treatment hit precisely the Germans who had suffered most from the Nazis and on whom we had to rely later as the new administrators. In the East, the Russian army sacked and looted the homes of workers, and in Berlin, particularly, violated German women of all ages. While, comparatively speaking, the Western armies behaved correctly, all that the Red Army did went into the four-power occupation account in the minds of the German people—a four-power alliance that according to its own proclamations to the German population, was intent on restoring democracy, law, and decency in the country where they had been destroyed by the Nazis. When our troops discovered the horror camps in Germany, we and the British forced the German people, whom we held collectively guilty for these outrages, to march by the mounds of dead bodies and to attend movie theatres where pictures of the camps were being shown. This was considered a small taste of punishment and the beginning of re-education. The comment of the Germans was that what they now saw only made it more plain to them

how impossible revolt would have been, and that any
attempt to revolt would have brought them to the
same fate. They were once more horrified by the evi-
dence of the utter degradation of their government
and the people by the totalitarian tyranny which now
lay buried under the ruins with all the life and wealth
it had destroyed. The Germans fully agree that these
horror camps were proof of the lowest depths to
which a society could sink, and they solemnly do pro-
fess their shame. But they ask you whether it is not
even more deplorable that now, four years after the
end of this horror regime and the victory of the democracies, concentration camps in the east which for
seven years the Nazis had filled with Germans and
thereafter also with nationals from other countries are
now overflowing once more with Germans who are
unwilling to knuckle under to the despotism of the
police state. They gladly point out that this is not true
in the three Western zones, but 17 million Germans
are subjected to the same tyranny as that of the Nazis,
under the auspices of the four powers which sat together at Nüremberg and rendered judgment on the
German people. Four-power control of Germany, do
not forget, officially broke down only in June, 1948.

If you point out that something had to be done to
punish those who were responsible for the murder of
millions of innocent people, and that an attempt was
made to lay foundations for a law with teeth in it to

prevent a recurrence of the same thing, the Germans will agree, and pause in silent meditation of the enormity of degradation in which they have been involved. For years, via newspapers, pamphlets, lectures, and the radio we have dinned into the German ear the verdict of collective guilt and have exhorted the people to repent and atone. The denazification procedures held every German guilty of participation in the crimes unless he could prove that he was not. This once more temporarily put on everyone a moral yellow tag and held each of them responsible for crimes organized and executed by the totalitarian tyranny which held them all tightly in its death grip.

But, as the conversation proceeds, the Germans will discuss the probability and the hope that foundations for a new start have been laid and that the evil will not just simply continue. Here the devil of faulty translation has played a trick on us. We have tried and convicted people at Nüremberg for "crimes against humanity," and our interpreters still translate this as "Verbrechen gegen die Menschlichkeit," which means "crimes against humaneness." Thus the Germans philosophize about "humaneness" in total war with its utter and total brutality and ask themselves if crimes against humaneness are punishable by death, as perhaps they ought to, and whether this criminal law is applicable also to the inhuman stripping of all their property, the expulsion and deportation of 10 million

men, women, and children from areas where their an-
cestors had worked and lived for centuries, hundreds of
these deportees arriving in the Western zones frozen to
death in freight cars. If you sidetrack this question by
pointing out that the Nazi regime brought the indig-
nation and wrath of the other nations to such a pitch
that at the end of the war such admittedly cruel policies
could not be prevented, they may inquire whether we
are really sincere in our condemnation of slave labor.
They will agree that drafting millions of slave laborers
from other countries was a crime and that Herr
Sauckel was justly hanged for it, but they also want to
know why, at Yalta, we condoned and agreed to the
use of German slave labor as one form of reparations,
and why not only the Russians but the Western
powers also have used German prisoners of war as
slave laborers for more than three years. They also ask
why we treated with respect the members of the Allied Control Council in Berlin who, several days after
Herr Sauckel was hanged, ordered 26,000 German
workers and their families drafted into Russia as slaves.

There is one solid block of good will in the hearts
of the German people which keeps alive their faith in
the reality of American democracy and counterbal-
ances a great many of the negative developments that
have occurred since the war. A flood of CARE and
SAFE packages and millions of privately packed relief
boxes of food and clothing sent by people all over this

country started for Germany as soon as the mails were opened up. The gratitude of the Germans for this spontaneous, active charity amounts to a sizable political asset in relations between them and the West. But it cannot make them soon forget that for prolonged periods the food rations in the Western zones fell to or below the rations fed the inmates of the Nazi horror camps.

I do not cite these extremely uncomfortable and unpleasant elements involved in discussions with Germans for the purpose of supporting their views; nor do I want to give the impression that Western occupation has not accomplished a great deal in reconstruction. I cite these matters because we must realize that much of what happened in Germany since the war's end has complicated the most important reconstruction job in Germany: the psychological and spiritual restoration of the nation.

There is still too much of the punitive and corrective periods of Western occupation permeating the third, ostensibly constructive phase of occupation policy. The youth of Germany particularly have gradually come out of their political coma, following the currency reform in June, 1948 and the loss of the fear of starving to death. More and more the people are beginning to take an active interest in domestic and foreign affairs. This is a healthy sign. Many foreign observers are alarmed by the manifestations of nationalism which sometimes accompany this active interest. For the most part, these expressions of nationalism are not objectionable, because they are only a symbol of the psychological process of self-preservation and self-protection by people who have gone through the most degrading phase of their national history and have been made to understand that all nations consider them collectively as outcasts. Being fenced off from the world, and having no choice but to carve out a living for their 50 million people within boundaries as confining as those of Great Britain, the Germans need a great deal of self-assurance in order not to despair. But it is quite obvious that within the next few years this political consciousness will be tested for its strength and for its elements of menace.

The time to avert the danger of strength turning into menace is now. The powerful energies inside Germany cannot forever be dammed up within this small area. They must be utilized for the benefit of the West-European community, and find further outlet in the freest flow of foreign trade into the world and the freest possible communication between Germans and other countries. If this is to be accomplished, the attitude of the occupying powers toward Germany must undergo radical change. It must be a radical and abrupt change, because the benefits to be expected from the change will not mature if it comes piecemeal and with such reluctance and delay that each step in it loses its stimulating effect. Provisional interim solutions like colonial status for the West State may seem to be a temporary convenience to some European governments, but they are no solution to the real problem, and if perpetuated will eventually cost the peace.

There are four principal steps that should be taken by the Western powers without equivocation:

(1) they should unilaterally declare peace with the West-German republic;

(2) they should grant economic sovereignty to the West-German republic;

(3) they should give the West-German republic the right of full membership in the Organization for European Economic Cooperation as envisaged in the April, 1949 agreement of the governments of the three Western powers;

(4) they should grant the West-German republic the right to establish official diplomatic and consular representation in foreign countries.

Economic sovereignty should be granted upon voluntary acceptance of certain temporary limitations and of a final settlement of reparations and restitution by the German government. Admission to the United Nations, though in principle desirable enough, does not make sense so long as its charter contains Article 107, which reads: [8]

---

[8] Carnegie Endowment for International Peace, *International Conciliation*, September, 1945, pp. 511-12.

Nothing in the present Charter shall invalidate or preclude action, in relation to any State which during the Second World War has been an enemy of any signatory to the present Charter, taken or authorized as a result of that war by the Governments having responsibility for such action.

This change in the Western attitude toward the German problem would lift the whole political thought on our part to an entirely different level, and would go a long way toward starting a new chapter in European history. It would draw a double line through the whole old account. It would terminate the policy of keeping Germany under quarantine, and it would open the gates for real European cooperation on a basis of fairness and mutual benefit.

The distinguished British economist, R. G. Hawtrey, in his book reporting the results of a prolonged and thorough study of Western European Union by a study group of the Royal Institute of International Affairs, stated: "*A union riven by distrust is no union. There is no escape from the conclusion that Western Germany must be admitted to a Western European Union on a footing of something like equality.*"[9]

Such a break with the past requires courage and imagination. It can be accomplished, but only by bold, constructive statesmanship on the part of the

---

[9] R. G. Hawtrey, *Western European Union; Implications for the United Kingdom* (Royal Institute of International Affairs, London and New York, 1949), p. 23. *Italics added.*

United States, Great Britain, and France. This change calls for continuous creative diplomatic labor on all sides—diplomacy that takes the initiative in developing and broadening avenues for international cooperation, and will keep the initiative throughout.

This policy would assure our taking the initiative away from the Soviets at last by consolidating a new and viable commonwealth of Western Europe that lived in peace and was strong. At the same time, the policy would change the psychological situation for the Germans in a most desirable sense from the standpoint of all her neighbors. It would rehabilitate the German people by a generous expression of confidence and forgiveness, and it would open more opportunities for their constructive contributions than they could possibly respond to. Instead of continually pressing against the host of barriers represented by allied prohibitions, supervisions, vetoes, ordinary red tape, and delay, the Germans would discover under the new commonwealth that their frontier was far wider than imagination or activity could digest. This state of affairs would be proper, not just for the German people, but for the sake of all the West-European nations. If they are all to hold their own in the wake of the vast Soviet empire with its planned economic expansion within the boundaries of Western Europe, they cannot do so by carrying on under a regime of more or less autarchic national economies. But if the

West-European nations manage to create the largest possible area of free exchange for goods, services, labor, capital, and "know-how," they could launch an era of economic expansion that could convert and absorb all the otherwise so destructive political energies of nationalism and radicalism of every sort into constructive economic endeavor.

France needs open economic frontiers as much as does Germany or Italy or any other nation of Western Europe. Continental economic expansion would be most beneficial to Great Britain. The practical step that should be taken to create these new opporunities is the application to other countries of the same sort of treaties as the one concluded last year between France and Italy concerning an economic union. If Germany could have a customs union with other West-European countries, particularly with France, both nations would eventually derive enormous benefit from it. If not only a customs union, but an economic union as well were achieved, Germany's industries would not only supplement those of France, and vice versa, but German experience, scientific research, and managerial ability would begin to stimulate French enterprise, at the same time that the German economy would receive the same impetus from French contributions. Moreover, so long as the area east of the Oder-Neisse rivers is cut off, Germany has such a vast food deficit that she could easily absorb the produce of France's entire excess agricultural capacity. The French four-year plan calls for the expansion of agricultural production to 125 per cent of prewar volume. In the equipment of European agriculture with modern tools and machinery, French, German, Belgian, Swiss, and Italian industries could, by division of labor and cooperation, curtail prices and obtain a reliable market with an increasing volume of demand.

So long as the attempt is made to integrate and expand the West-European economy by exploiting as long as possible the position of the victors over the Germans under the guise of military security, the only result will be that the Germans will become more nationalistic and less inclined to cooperate. National socialism in Germany got its first boost in 1923 when the French army occupied the Ruhr to force the export of coal to France as reparations. If raised to the position of an equal partner in a new Europe, the West-German republic's citizens will prove to be able and inspiring cooperators, the more so since the old delusions of grandeur are gone.

But by an agreement of December 28, 1948[10] the United States, Great Britain, France, and the Benelux countries have imposed an international authority on the main industrial area of Germany, the so-called "Ruhr." Germany is no party to this agreement. The

---

[10] U. S. Dept. State, *Department of State Bulletin*, Jan. 9, 1949, pp. 43-52.

Government of the future German West State can accede to the agreement by voluntarily shouldering the obligations imposed by the signatory powers, but it cannot thereby become a signatory, and will be excluded from the procedures for alteration or termination of the agreement. In the Council of the Ruhr Authority the signatory powers have twelve votes (the United States, Great Britain, and France three each; the Benelux countries one each), while, if it should accede to the agreement, the West-German republic will have three. The council is empowered to allocate specific amounts and quality grades of coal, coke, and steel to export and domestic usage and to supervise production, investment, and development. The United States, Great Britain, France, and Belgium are all heavy producers of coal, coke, and steel. The power to restrict the amount of coal, coke, and steel for domestic use is the power to restrict the reconstruction of Germany and to control nearly all industrial developments.

In the six-power communiqué about the agreement, it is stated that while the six governments are determined to prevent a recurrence of the use of the resources of the Ruhr for purposes of aggression, "they are equally aware that the political and economic welfare of Europe requires the full and effective use of the industrial production of the Ruhr and the participation of a democratic Germany in the comity of

nations, all enjoying a reasonable standard of prosperity." The communiqué continues: "The establishment of the Ruhr Authority is an innovation in the
international economic field. It is not being set up to
limit free competition by European industries in the
markets of the world. It has a constructive function
to fulfill in promoting the general economic wellbeing of Europe and in re-establishing international
confidence. If operated wisely, the Ruhr Authority
may be regarded as a further contributory step to-
wards a more intimate economic association among the
countries of Europe."[11]

Earlier, it is stated that the Ruhr Authority shall be
one of the means by which a peaceful democratic
Germany can be brought into the European comity
to play its part as a fully responsible and independent
member. In spite of such avowed noble sentiments,
the fact remains that the Ruhr Authority further ac-
centuates the future German government's extremely
limited authority within its most vital area of economic concern. In the absence of an arbitration court
or other court of review, the door is left wide open for
interference with the German economy. That interference in effect will amount to protection of the
victors from competition in foreign trade and will
deny the vanquished the opportunity for ever gaining

---

[11] U. S. Dept. State, *Department of State Bulletin*, Jan. 9, 1949,
p. 44.

a sufficient volume of trade to pay their food-import bill. The signatory powers have given no hint of any desire to extend the principles of the Ruhr Authority to the French or Belgian coal and steel resources, which obviously are by nature equally important to the wellbeing of the European comity. If an expansion of this sort of international supervision of vital resources were attempted, the German case would lose its resemblance to a crippling device employed against a democratic government by six nations whose economic prosperity is closely tied in with the exploitation of native coal and iron resources.

It is conceivable that the Council of the Ruhr Authority may use its great power in a spirit of fairness and wisdom, but it is forseeable also that the inevitable hardships the German people will have to endure for many years will induce them to blame the Authority and to suspect a revival of Morgenthauism in its actions. Politically, this fencing in of German authority from its most vital area once bred a dangerous brand of nationalism, and could do so again.

If the new German government should accede to the agreement, and thus voluntarily recognize and submit to an arrangement by which the victors deliberately fetter it within its most vital economic sphere, accession may well lead to the doom of the political careers and leadership of the men composing this government. If the government refuses to accede,

and thereby demonstrates what the six exclusive sig-
natories to the Authority would undoubtedly call
"non-cooperation," the situation would prove every
bit as embarrassing from the standpoint of establishing
a vital peace in Western Europe.

As it stands, the Ruhr Authority is one further
measure that prohibits the integration of Germany
into Western Europe. Since its origin lies chiefly in
the insistent demand of the French for effective security against Germany, the Ruhr Authority should
be obviated by a treaty for closest economic cooperation between France and Germany, in which the Benelux countries and Italy could also join. In his Zürich
address of September 19, 1946 on a United States of
Europe, Winston Churchill said: "I am now going to
say something which will astonish you. The first step
in the re-creation of the European family must be a
partnership between France and Germany. In this
way only can France recover the moral and cultural
leadership of Europe. There can be no revival of
Europe without a spiritually great France and a spiritually great Germany." In conclusion, he stressed this
theme again by saying, "In all this urgent work, France
and Germany must take the lead together."[12]

The integration of Germany into Western Europe
cannot be confined to some sort of economic cooperation. Concluding trade treaties, customs unions, and

---

[12] *Vital Speeches of the Day*, Oct. 1, 1946, p. 742.

even economic unions with the free movement of capital and labor, desirable as they are, will not of itself create a new and vital European commonwealth of nations. Political integration, while tremendously difficult, must still be the long-run goal. Indeed, some of the economic treaties will not be concluded at all unless prior political understanding has been reached. Provisions may well be made, even, for a permanent council of foreign ministers holding regular meetings, and for other councils made up of cabinet members of various countries with the same portfolios. Discussion, exchange of views, and attempts to find larger areas of agreement on cooperative action in various fields of governmental policy would certainly be a long step toward conciliation and the construction of a better atmosphere for international relations. Here again, the Germans as well as the Italians, can make exceptional contributions. Both of these countries have gone through the bitter collapse of democracy succeeded by the totalitarian state. They recognize every one of the dead-end streets of democracy as well as all the dangers of panaceas. Labor and management in both countries have learned a great deal from the past 25 years, and the relations between the two seem to me— perhaps not generally—but in a great many cases to be on a more advanced level than in other Western countries. The promotion of social peace and progress in Europe would in any case profit from the exchange of thought and experience on the question of labor-management relations.

Economic integration without at least a maximum of genuine political cooperation among equals is a fiction. But as soon as we begin to envisage even a very modest scope of political integration, the most crucial acute, and complex issue of all takes precedence—the military defense of Western Europe.

The people of Western Europe today live in deadly fear of the Russian army, its enormous number of armored divisions and infantry divisions that are stationed just behind the Iron Curtain, poised to move westward at a moment's notice. It is generally assumed that these armored divisions could reach the Rhine in 24 hours and the Atlantic coast in another 48, notwithstanding some well-equipped American and British constabulary forces. The military forces in most of Western Europe amount to little more than national police forces, equipped to quell attempts at coups d'état or riots by domestic radical groups. Not one of them presents any serious problem to the tanks of the Red Army. The only exception to that is the Swiss army, which is the largest national army in Europe, by far the best equipped on the Continent, and it has a superb morale. Combined with its formidable defense system in the Alps, its personnel and weapons offer some real protection against being summarily swept up in an armored drive. The Brussels agreement on a joint staff for the defense of France, the Benelux countries, and Great Britain was the first step, and the Atlantic Pact among the 10 West-European nations, the United States, and Canada was the second step toward erecting a bulwark of collective military security for Western Europe against aggression. Germany has been left out of both efforts, but it was announced last fall that the plans for the military defense of Western Europe drawn up by the joint command under Viscount Montgomery provided for the defense of the Rhine.

This announcement had a negative effect, to put it mildly, upon the German population east of the Rhine, because they felt that in the event of war they would be left in a no-man's land in front of that imaginary line, which would stop tank columns even less effectively than the Maginot Line had done. Indeed, as if with intended irony, it was added by radio that the German population would have to defend itself as best it could. The possession of firearms or munitions by any German is a serious criminal offense against the armies of occupation. On this point, Professor Hawtrey stated:[13]

> It is obvious that a Western European Union cannot afford to surrender the industries of the Ruhr and Rhine valleys to hostile occupation; it must prepare to defend the territory which contains them.

---

[13] R. G. Hawtrey, *op. cit.*, pp. 22-23.

Defence of a disarmed Germany by armies of occupation, in the semblance of a colonial dependency, is
hardly a proposal to be entertained. An ally distrust of
which is openly proclaimed and given concrete shape
in enforced disarmament, is not likely to be reliable.

The 20-year North Atlantic Pact, now up for
ratification, requires the immediate placement of a
sufficient supply of defense weapons on the Continent.
Unless that requirement is met, the pact is worse than
no alliance at all. If we have nothing better to offer to
the nations of Western Europe in the event of their
swift occupation by a motorized aggressor than eventually a few planes carrying atomic bombs, we cannot
hope to relieve them from their fear.

But suppose that we do ratify the Atlantic Pact, irrespective of the Soviet attempts to lull us for awhile into a state of false security, and suppose that we supply
the arms to build an adequate defense system in Western Europe. It still does not settle the political question of whether it is the task of each nation to build and
maintain its own national army and to participate only
in plans for joint operations in case of emergency.
Separate armies in each of the West-European nations
is no solution to the problem of building an effective
modern defense system; moreover, individual national
armies would become a strong deterrent to the expansion of the European economy. There could be no
stronger or more healthy influence upon genuine inte-

gration of the nations of Western Europe than the construction, on a cooperative basis, of a strong, common defense system. Ideally, such a defense system would consist of national quotas, a joint command, and a system for rotating the elements of the army among the actual defense stations. Such a force could be developed to a highly efficient and reliable unit in which all participants could take just pride. As the tri-lingual Swiss army has demonstrated, language differences present no serious obstacle to efficient performance.

If this were the basis for the defense of Western Europe, there would be no compelling reason why a German quota could not be admitted to this army after a period of two years or so. At the present time, the German people have no desire to see the restoration of a German army. Every third man between 20 and 40 years of age is dead, and there is a ratio of 17 women to 10 men in that age group. The Germans say, "Count me out if you are planning for an army." They are consoled by and are even anxious to have the occupation troops remain in the country for purposes of military security. If, instead of the armies of the United States, Great Britain, and France, plus small Belgian, Dutch, and Danish units, there were installed a part of a joint European army, with the eventual participation of a German quota provided for, the Germans would accept it. In fact, the constitution for the West-German state specifically transfers the task of national defense to a European federation.

In the long run, the solution of the military issue must be sought in the voluntary surrender of that part of national sovereignty that permits each nation to maintain an autarchic defense system, in exchange for participation in a common European defense system. Then the alternative of either permanent demilitarization or the restoration of the German army would lose its meaning. The adoption and prompt execution of a new policy of restoring economic and political sovereignty at once, as the necessary prerequisite to Germany's integration into the West-European community, would have so revolutionary an effect that the change in the country's defense status could probably be postponed for a considerable length of time.

It seems utopian to believe that it will be possible to keep Germany permanently occupied by foreign armies. To do so would engender political insecurity and vitiate any genuine conciliation among the people of Western Europe. Security can be created only by intelligent and fair cooperation with the best economic and political leaders in Western Germany, by assigning to the German people tasks that will constructively contribute to the welfare of Western Europe, and by progressively eliminating the conditions which breed distress and dissatisfaction. At the present time there is a considerable amount of abuse of power by the military occupation which must come to an end as quickly as possible. Disguised as military security, many vetoes, industrial restrictions, and dismantling orders in reality strive for security against German competition in the world's markets. The Humphrey committee has pointed out, in this connection, that a too low level of German industrial activity is a much more serious threat to peace than a too-productive German industry.

So long as no new approach is made to find a Continental solution to the West-European defense problem, and so long as nothing else is done except to rebuild a dozen Continental armies, those armies will prove to be the cancer that will destroy the tissue of a new Europe. Economic integration may make no progress at all, because national armies always consider any international division of labor to be dangerous.

Never before in the world's bloody history have the opportunities for uniting and reconciling the peoples of Europe been as great as they are today. The common jeopardy to all of them—victors, liberated, and vanquished alike—makes them inclined to think about a new cooperative approach to the problem of common defense and a common construction of peace. While many routine politicians over there continue to play the old records of the 1920's and 1930's all over again, there is a surprising number of others—young and old alike—who are inspired by the vision of a Europe restored to its earlier spiritual and cultural unity, given a solid material foundation by a new era of economic cooperation and rising production.

The ultimate solution of the German problem in a Western sense is the moot point for European cooperation of any sort. Our American contribution to this cooperation should be the use of our influence to bring about real conciliation between Germany and her Western neighbors—at once, and the purchase of a broad flow of German export goods and services. Not only should universities, colleges, professional societies, churches, and civic groups restore friendly relations with German groups and individuals, visit them and invite them to this country, but even greater efforts should be made to foster multiangular relations throughout Western Europe. After everything that has happened, and with the situation as it has been shaped by the occupation powers up to now, the initiative cannot come from the Germans, no matter how good their record or how great their merits may be. It is up to us to begin anew and to do our part to reintegrate Germany into the Western World.

There is no longer the isolated problem of Germany. The real problem is one of establishing a vital peace through world-wide economic expansion. The key to such a peace in Europe, however, lies in Germany.